Unhindered

A Journey to Move with Power and Purpose

JEANA LINDBERT

WestBow
PRESS
A DIVISION OF THOMAS NELSON

WestBow Press books may be ordered through booksellers or by contacting:

WestBow Press
A Division of Thomas Nelson
1663 Liberty Drive
Bloomington, IN 47403
www.westbowpress.com
1-(866) 928-1240

ISBN: 978-1-4497-8777-6 (sc)
ISBN: 978-1-4497-8776-9 (e)
ISBN: 978-1-4497-8778-3 (hc)

Library of Congress Control Number: 2013904162

Printed in the United States of America

WestBow Press rev. date: 4/4/2013

Table of Contents

Introduction

This book was written to inspire people to move with power and purpose through Jesus Christ, whose movement has changed lives for thousands of years. We are all capable of and responsible for moving in a mighty, holy way as we have learned from our Savior. May He inspire us to step out of what we know and feels safe into an unstoppable faith that follows God wherever He leads.

"The risk of regret is greater than the fear of failure."

1

Cereal Anyone?

It was a Monday morning and the first day back to school. The music played loudly in my head as the horse's hooves approached. Yes, the race was on. Not planning to admit defeat, I continued on, unwilling to surrender. Clothes were laid out the night before, leaving the only decision as to whether the kids would brush their teeth before or after breakfast.

As the early morning sun peered through the windows, I walked down the hall to find my boys running around their rooms, bouncing off beds and, yes, getting dressed in their uniforms, belts, shoes, and even socks. They were enthusiastic for the first day back to school, and I was frenzied, trying to make sure everything went smoothly.

Leaving them to their own devices, I ran downstairs to prepare a breakfast made for a king, or, at the very least, four princes. Pots clanged, utensils flew, and heat rose from the stove as I made breakfast and lunches all at once. This was a piece of cake; I had it under control, no problem.

Three of my four boys thumped down the stairs like a small

herd of elephants while I threw together whatever somewhat-healthy items I could find for their lunches. What had I done? I had planned breakfast so specifically that I had somehow forgotten to stock up on lunch supplies! Birthday parties, soccer games, church events, and a social prevented me from going to the grocery store over the weekend, but surely I could find something.

Creativity kicked in. As I worked out who would get the last orange, the overly ripe banana, and who may not get a piece of fruit that day, I whisked the eggs, stirred the hash browns, and placed the biscuits on a baking sheet and the grits on the stove (yes, we are from the South). I was in the zone. You know, one of those "Mother of the Year" moments. They were already making my plaque. This was a memory my boys would hold onto forever. They would tell their grandkids about the time their mom made them an elaborate breakfast with all the fixings, beautiful flowers on the table, no paper plates, and all before their first day of school. Okay, so that was not completely honest. There were flowers on the table, but they were brown and wilted and should have been thrown away days earlier. But the rest was true, and breakfast was going to be magical.

While breakfast was nearing completion, I remembered that my youngest son, Asher, was still sleeping. I ran upstairs, scooped him into my arms, and brought him back downstairs and laid him on the couch so he, too, could partake in the feast prepared in his brothers' honor. I rushed back to the stove to finish stirring and checking.

My boys huddled on the couch with the early-morning, excitement-wearing-off daze plastered on their faces. I saw them but honestly had no time to look up. This was going to be the greatest meal ever. As I continued working, the more proud I became. I thought about other boys and girls and how

I was certain their parents weren't doing all this for their first day back to higher education with the quest to fuel their brains. I felt even more proud that I was doing this all by myself as my husband left early that morning for work. Can you hear the horn playing and all for me?

While my boys waited patiently, even quietly, my oldest son, Jacob, said to me, "Mommy, look at me." I told him to wait, that I had big things I was doing. Again he declared, "Mommy, look at me!"

I abruptly said, "Wait!"

Are you kidding me? I thought to myself. He was so ungrateful and demanding while I was sweating over this amazing meal.

I was frantic at this point, with only fifteen minutes before we had to leave for school. Everything would be ready to come out and off in the next minute. Let's face it; boys eat fast, so this would be easy. Come on. One more minute and I can sit for a second before we are off to school. Then Jacob spoke loudly, passionately, and boldly as he said for the third time, "Mom, please look at me!"

Exasperated, with spatula in hand and with only thirty seconds on the clock, I looked straight into his big, brown, doe-like eyes as they bore into mine. "What?!"

With a smile and in a voice as gentle as a whisper, Jacob said, "I needed you to look up so you could see how much I love you."

The spatula hit the ground and the timer went off, but the only thing my body would allow me to do in that moment was grab my child. My heart melted as my sweet little boy simply needed me to look at him so I could see how much he loved me. It just doesn't get any better than that.

We all sat in a pile and snuggled for the next few minutes.

We didn't worry about the crazy day ahead. We didn't think about anything else but each other. No "Mother of the Year" award, no fancy breakfast, no amazing words that were going to change the universe. The only thing I could utter from my quivering lips was, "I love you all so much!"

In my quest to be the perfect mom, I almost failed my family that morning. By some standards, maybe I did. What I do know is that my child was persistent, a character trait he still carries, and I looked up. In my efforts toward greatness, I lost sight of why I was trying to be great. It began for my boys, but it became about me. I needed to hurry up and slow down.

I walked with my boys through the kitchen, gave them each a bottle of water, turned off the timer that was still beeping along with the stove, and grabbed an entire box of cereal that would be their breakfast in the car ride to school. My youngest was still in his pajamas, and we loaded up with backpacks in tow and off we went.

Wow, what a flop. My bubble burst, but my children were happy and absolutely fine with chomping dry cereal as we made our way to school. We all had smiles on our faces and a song in our heart. In that moment, I thanked God as I have never thanked Him before. I remember it to this day; it is forever marked. I reflected on His presence, gave each of my boys a big hug for a big day, and waved until I thought my arm would fall off. My children loved me and, oh, how I loved them.

As I drove away from school with my little pajama boy, all I could think about was how amazing God was and is. How amazing that we get to see His love each day if we only open our eyes and our hearts to it. I noticed the hues of green that painted the trees, the grass, and the bushes. The flowers were shades of blues, yellows, and purples that went beyond the spectrum and greater than my imagination. The sky was as blue as the ocean with animal-shaped clouds floating through its waves. The birds soared through the air like horses galloping to their stables. God did all this so we could see how much He loves us.

All these things had new life as I reflected on what God has given us to show His care and love. With intricacy and precision, He has given us things that speak of His love while showing it at the same time.

Wow, how powerful that moment, ingraining itself into my soul. God is so good and available; His presence is in the life He has breathed into His creations.

Then it hit me. Wait a minute. I am one of those creations! God, so gracious, merciful, and loving to lift me up in His arms and hug me as only a Father can, held me that morning as a tear trailed down my cheek. I thought about how blessed I am to be a child of the Father greater than any other, the Creator of absolute beauty, a mighty King.

How many times had I missed it? How many times had He or someone else tugged at my sleeve to get me to see or hear or be part of something great? We can all get so busy that we forget to stop and simply look up.

We live hurried lives and feel better about ourselves when we say we are busy. We live in an overindulged, over-enticed, and over-expectant society. Maybe it makes us feel important or special or needed. I can be the first on that list, so I am casting no stones. I am just tired of rushing and feeling like I have to. Tired of being concerned about what others think. Tired of wondering whether they like me. Tired of wishing I measured up. Tired, just tired, of being busy. We listen to the lie that if we are going, going, going, people will be in awe of all that we accomplish, even if we are left empty and dry at the end of the day. We think if something isn't working or going as expected, we can simply find something better, perhaps a new job, a new relationship, or a new responsibility.

Being on the go is a self-made societal phenomenon. It enables people to avoid or deny their problems, make excuses for neglect, and implode upon themselves. It is a destructive way to live. If we don't start listening, the voice that is calling us to look up may just stop speaking.

Someone is calling you. You have a choice to stay busy or hurry up and slow down. Yes, you have a choice to see the One who has been calling you all along. Even Jesus, our greatest example, looked up. When He raised Lazarus from the dead, John 11:41–44 NLT says,

"So they rolled the stone aside. Then Jesus looked up to heaven and said, "Father, thank you for hearing me. You always hear me, but I said it out loud for the sake of all these people standing here, so that they will believe you sent me." Then Jesus shouted, "Lazarus, come out!" And the dead man came out..."

God needed His Son to look up as an example to others. Jesus is always calling us to come out and is willing to raise us from the dead where we busy ourselves with mindless, useless activity.

There are surely things that must get done. Some mundane tasks are necessary for the structure of our lives, but they are not mindless activities. The useless activities are those things that rob us of being all we are supposed to be and steal our joy. Jesus is pressing in and pushing us away from such things, calling us to come alive. In His life exists the power and purpose of the God movement breathing within us that needs resurrecting and new direction. God is ready for us to look up, come out, and be ready for the greatest journey of our lives.

The movement of God isn't about you; it is about Him. It took me awhile to figure that out. I finally realized that I am no superhero. I am not perfect. I don't do most things right. But one thing I learned on that Monday morning is that I want to be the mom, wife, daughter, child, and woman who looks up.

I may not be able to make a breakfast feast, and I may not be able to do it all. But I can be okay with the Me that I can be. That doesn't give me license to be lazy, but it does give me license to embrace grace and know that I am only human. I will make mistakes and trials will come, but triumphs will be even brighter, love will be stronger, and life will go on whether my children are having eggs or cereal. I am now okay that when I can't do it all, can't have it all, and can't be it all, I will simply say, "Cereal anyone? Eggs are made by superheroes."

2

Superheroes Move

Superheroes are birthed out of our desperate need for a savior, when we need to be rescued and brought to safety. In the movies, superheroes walk in the skin of a human being while bolstering extreme powers. They are simple yet somehow complex beings. When there is a damsel in distress, a child trapped in a burning building, or a bus hanging off the side of a cliff, the superhero swoops in and saves the day. There is always a way for him to rescue, whether by flying, swinging, or running.

Superheroes were created so our action-seeking minds could see what being saved in the flesh looks like. How interesting that the price has already been paid; the rescuer has already reached out His hand and has saved the day as no earthly superhero can. Seeing the lost brought into allegiance with the hope and grace that can only be offered by that of a real superhero is quite incredible.

Sure, watching movies with heroes is fun with their masks, capes, outfits, and superpowers. It is a fantasy world we can enter when life is too heavy to bear, an escape from reality.

Clearly, no man in a red cape is going to take me flying with him above the clouds. No man in a spider suit is going to web his way to pick me up when I am down. No monstrous, green humanoid is going to break through walls to come to my aid, and no man with long golden locks is going to smash a hammer to the ground for the Earth's axis to change on my behalf. In truth, it is all sort of silly, but, oh, how we love to enter the world of make-believe. The place where all the wrongs are made right, the enemy is defeated, and the good guys always win.

But guess what? We are living that, and we get to be part of it. Jesus is our superhero. He is always available to rescue and save. That is what He does. No red cape or costume necessary. He is perfection come down from heaven. He is our hero and is waiting each day to heal and deliver us. Just as He called Lazarus to come out of the tomb, He calls us to rise up. He isn't concerned whether we can make a breakfast feast or have completed fifty things in one day. He cares about our heart and our willingness to move as He calls.

God loves us and gave us the perfect gift of His Son so we could understand the righteousness we have been offered. Grace, love, hope, and mercy have been poured out so we might see the possibilities of a new day. This life isn't about comic book characters; it is about the One who truly gave so we might live. He wants us to live with purpose and, most of all, movement.

Now please hear me. This is not a judgment against the superheroes of the world. No way! I enjoy them too. They take me to new places and free me for a moment in time, like the world stands still while the heroes fight and I just sit and watch. Funny, though, when the movie is over, the same things that were happening in my life before the movie are still happening.

I have to awaken to the life-giving power of Christ that is within me and be empowered with that. Trusting in God is my strength. Faith is my rescuer. Hope is my healing. God sent His Son to be the superhero of this world. He also has given us everything we will ever need to be a hero in the lives of those we encounter here on earth. He didn't give us a spirit of laziness because that isn't in Him. He didn't give us a spirit of pride because that isn't a part of Him. We weren't given fear because fear never lived in Him. Jesus gave us a spirit of power—quite possibly the power of a superhero because we have been given the power of the King, which will invade every place in our lives like a military force on the frontline, impacting and transforming future movements.

Have you ever missed the movement? You know, the moment when God placed an opportunity right in front of you and you passed it by, ignored it, or allowed anxiety to debilitate you. I have. More than once. However, one moment stands out in my mind.

Every morning, I drove by a mother and her children standing at a bus stop. The mom always glowed with joy as she talked and laughed with her children. Her beauty as a woman and as a mother always made me smile. She was clearly enamored by her little ones and patiently waited by their side until the bus arrived. After months and months of watching from afar the sweet spirit that flowed over that family, I noticed that the woman became less active and more withdrawn.

Then I saw the bandana over what was once shoulder-length, sandy brown hair. "No, God! Take the cancer away!" I said out loud as I drove by her. "Take this from her, from this woman I do not know. Do not allow this cancer to even breathe within her." Tears streamed down my cheeks for this incredible woman I had never met. Yet somehow I did know her. I knew she loved her children, and I wanted desperately for her to have life.

From that moment on, I only saw her a few times. She looked pale but still always wore a smile. I am sure some days offered more strength than others. She was a reminder for me to live every day to the fullest. I knew I had to make a difference in the lives of those around me.

About two months later, I noticed a bit of hair growth when I drove past her, and I praised God, as I assumed she must be healing. Yet something dark came over me, a feeling of oppression and pain. Then the Holy Spirit told me to stop my car in the middle of the road and pray over this woman I had never met. The urge within me was so strong it hurt. My body ached, and I became physically ill. However, I couldn't stop. She would think I was crazy! She didn't know me. How could I stop my car and just pray over a woman who, by all outward appearances, was getting better? My decision to not stop ate away at me for days, even weeks.

I didn't tell anyone at the time about this experience, as I knew I had disobeyed God's movement in my life. I thought about that woman, her family, and her health, but I never saw her again. Wondering if she had moved and was healed, I sought any information about her I could.

Finally, I found someone who could tell me what had become of that lovely woman who exhibited such grace. In a somber, flat tone, they told me her story, and my throat tightened, my eyes blurred with tears, and my heart broke. The beautiful, joy-filled woman who loved her children and life had lost her battle with cancer and had passed away.

I immediately realized that I had passed her by. I had ignored God and did not become part of the movement He had so clearly placed before me. I am not saying that my prayer would have changed anything, for that would be self-righteous. However, I wasn't obedient and sold out. I was more concerned with looking silly than I was with following the plan God so clearly had placed before me. His movement was all over me, but I became paralyzed by fear of rejection. Instead, I should have willingly walked out the movement God had set in motion within me, which had a certain purpose and, through God, divine power. "Oh, God, help me to not just sit next time You call. I choose to be a part of Your movement."

Second Timothy 1:7 tells us, "For God has not given us a spirit of fear and timidity, but of power, love, and self-discipline" (emphasis added). God didn't create us to sit on the sidelines and be a spectator in this life. We have been given a colossal opportunity to impact and change this world for the cause of Christ. We have abilities unlike any other, skills, talents, and gifts that God has entrusted to us. We are alive! The question is, will we lay down all that holds us back to be all that God has made us to be?

God has given us everything we need and has made us capable. In following God's plan and stepping out in extreme faith, we will sometimes feel uncomfortable. When we get off the couch and move toward a cause, we are no longer safe. The defining moment is when we step out of the box that has enclosed us for far too long and are ready to embrace the plan God has designed specifically with us in mind.

We will find ourselves in uncomfortable places when we are not held back any longer. When we rise up in faith, we should feel most at home in those uncomfortable places as children of God, for there is where we will find God's purpose flow over our lives.

So throw the doubt, fear, hopelessness, shame, pride, and death away, shout for Satan to get behind you, and run forward with all the might and strength given to you by a Holy God. He has come to save the day! He is ready to deliver you, rescue you, and pull you out of the rubbish you have been lying in for far too long. Stand up! Get ready for the journey that will encourage you to be more than you are in this moment. You will receive strength and will feel the love, the perfect love, of your Savior.

On an afternoon that looked like any other at our house, activity was exploding everywhere. Two of my boys were racing in the front yard, one was searching for bugs, and one was busy feeling the plush, green grass under his knees as his crawling adventures had only just begun. My oldest son, Jacob, continuously won in the races with his younger brother, Levi, which seemed unfair, but who was I to intervene? Finally, the frustration rose to a new level, and after losing for the fifth time, Levi said two simple words that have unfortunately dictated much of our society, "I quit!"

What came next made me laugh and forced me to reflect upon the human spirit. Jacob quickly noticed Levi's defeated attitude and said, "Way to go, Levi! I am a winner, but you are a winner too!"

Confused, Levi asked, "How?"

Jacob remarked, "Well, I won the race. But you won too. You are the first place loser!" Levi smiled, not quite understanding the weight of such a comment. And Jacob had no idea as to the gravity in his statement either. He truly thought he was encouraging his brother.

Isn't it funny how a statement can mark our self-proclaimed destiny? Of course, we have taught Levi that he is not a loser and Jacob to be more cautious with his words. However, what happens when we don't have someone to detour us from negative talk or the course that could quite possibly be a road of self-destruction?

Quitting is not an option. Jesus never quit on us but kept moving in the direction that caused Him great pain but ended in greater triumph. Jesus showed us what we are capable of when we follow God.

The human spirit is resilient and powerful. Think about it like this. If you stretch a rubber band as far as it will go and gently bring it back until there is no tension, it will go back to the form in which you started. However, stretching a rubber band and then letting go of one side can hurt someone. In the same way, the human spirit fights with the Holy Spirit for control over who you are.

You have listened to the flesh for too long. It is time to let go gently and allow the life-breathing peace to take over your life. Let go of control, and release the power back to the One to whom it belongs. When you offer your willing spirit, you open yourself up for God's leading that will quite possibly knock your socks off. That movement is in itself the very definition of a hero.

Seek Him and talk to Him, as He is always listening, standing in your place, and closing the gap. Praying is our greatest access to our Father. Just as you nourish your relationship with a friend or spouse by communicating with him or her, so it should be with God. He knows your heart's desires and wants to fulfill them. Even if it seems like God isn't coming through for you and you feel desperate and discouraged, He is still there. These are honest, real emotions, but God will never stop delighting in you. Don't give up; you can't quit. You must move and continue believing that God has every good thing intended for your life. Keep talking to Him.

Likewise, He has written the most beautiful story ever told.

His book explains your destiny, dreams, and purpose. Read His Word, the Bible, and explore and live it. The Bible is like the blood that courses through our veins, and prayer is like oxygen to our bodies. Without talking to God and reading His Word, we can't fully understand His plan, nor can we fully live. When in constant communication with Him, we can recognize that defining moment when all that God has for us becomes clear, our focus shifts, and His glory is revealed.

We spin our wheels reading self-help books, listening to thought-provoking talks meant to change our lives for the better, and watching shows with hosts who seem to know every intricate detail of how to heal someone's life from the inside out. The truth is, while those things have great intentions, many even pure, the Bible is the only book, God is the only speaker, and Jesus is the only healer who can truly transform your life. The purpose of this book is to spur you onward toward the movement God has intended for you. God defines you, and that definition is full of life, love, and purpose that only He can provide.

The superheroes of the world have a power within them to rescue those who need saving. However, we, too, have all the power we need to charge the world with the same force and energy as any masked, caped superhero, for we have been given the power and purpose of our Creator. The Holy Spirit is the living power within us that fuels our muscles and bones, our minds and hearts, to bring synergy and pulse to our every movement. So look up, keep moving, and know that the power you need to change the world lives inside you through Jesus Christ.

3

To Bee in Control

Have you ever held something so closely that it hurt? Have you ever gripped something or someone so tight, maybe your children, dreams, money, guilt, or pain, that you forgot how to live freely? The sting can confuse or even wound you and produce such trauma that your next move is actually no move at all.

When we hold someone or some things with white-knuckled, clenched fists, we are trying to claim control that in actuality we do not have. The problem with control is that it has more power over us than we have over it. Holding people or things too tightly will suffocate and snuff the very life out of them.

The bee buzzed around the stroller, oblivious to the fact that he was far inferior to the one-year-old within it. My child joyfully waved at all the cars and people passing by as I pushed his stroller down the storefront sidewalk. We were out for fresh air and to take in the beauty around us.

The bee continued buzzing around my child's head. I believed that my best action in this case was no action; just ignore it, it will go away. So I continued walking. And the bee continued hovering. Maybe my child smelled sweet from the banana he had eaten minutes earlier. Whatever the case, surely the bee would cause no harm.

Well, I was wrong. The bee was determined, almost on the attack. My son rested his hand on the side of his stroller. Thinking this was a fun game, he giggled when the bee crawled on his arm. I shooed it away, but it returned and landed directly in my son's palm. I couldn't react fast enough. Before I could swat at the bee or tell my son to move his hand, he closed his fingers into his palm, catching the bee.

As you can imagine, the bee was none too happy and dug his stinger into my one-year-old's hand. Asher quickly opened his hand, and the bee just fell, dazed and confused. However, my son was crying, and his hand swelled. I pulled out the stinger, but of course it didn't make the pain disappear. Asher eventually settled down, and even though the sting affected him for a couple of days, he was fine.

This experience made me realize what happens when we hold things too tightly. I can be an absolute control freak at times and am very involved in my children's lives. I want to know their happenings and have my hand on what takes place in their lives. While I absolutely believe it is our responsibility as parents to be on top of our children's movements, there were times when I was snuffing the life out of them, unwilling to give them enough room to make their own mistakes.

My controlling ways moved into my work and even into some of my other relationships. I am embarrassed to say that I have lived much of my life by the saying, "If you want something done right, do it yourself." But many of my life experiences have contributed to this belief. I know all too well that when we give someone a task and they don't come through, it hurts, and that when we are hurt, oftentimes we shut down and revert to our own devices. Whatever the situation, I have lived trying to claim control, only to finally realize that I really have none.

Control is believing we have command or authority over something or someone when in actuality we don't. We don't have control over our lives or anyone else's. Sure, we make decisions that take us down one path or another. Yet there is a greater force that holds us back from full surrender to God. Laying things down is easier said than done. The payoff for not laying it down is control.

I have learned that holding people or things too tightly leaves no room for life. When we clench our fists, we get stung. Control is not a part of movement but is a place of pain and even death. God movements are not about control but rather relinquishing control to the Father, who knows what is best, and trusting Him with the results.

When it comes to God things, we must let the sand fall freely. We must loosen our grip so people and things can breathe. There is no growth when someone or something can't gain ground and get air. If we hold onto guilt, shame, fear, doubt, rejection, or the past, we slowly drain the life out of our own being. God is on our side and wants prosperity, hope, and peace for us. He knows the longing of our hearts, for they are His.

God has loved us with an irreplaceable love from the beginning of time. Before we were in our mother's womb, He called us His. His eyes are always on us, and His affection is poured upon us. His adoration is filling us even now. God will ride in on His white horse to rescue and save and will wipe out all the Enemy's oppressive lies and tactics. So unclench your fists, and allow the movement to sift gently through your fingers. Allow resurrection in your spirit so you can move.

Remember how much you are loved, forgiven, and redeemed by way of the cross. Jesus died so you could be free. Knowing that, why waste another day with any falsehoods the Enemy throws at you? You have been bought with the blood of Jesus, and nothing you do or have done can change that. Jesus' last words were, "It is finished!" as stated in John 19:30. He didn't say, "Only some of it is finished" or "I am only partially done here" or "I did this for only a few." No, He said, "It is finished," and He meant for all.

Everything you have done or ever will do was placed on Him that day. As His body was beaten, mocked, ripped, and torn, He thought of you. No sting in the palm could compare to that. He felt the love His Father had for you, which allowed Him to endure incomprehensible pain. He was the King of all kings, yet He wore a crown of thorns that dripped with the perfect blood of a Savior. His side bore the gaping wound inflicted by a soldier who thought his life was more valuable than that of God in the flesh. His feet bore the nail that held the weight of our sins as He lifted Himself for hours simply to breathe. His hands, oh, the sweet, gentle hands that touched people, healed many, and gave much as a carpenter, teacher, and Savior, were held back that day on a block of wood so that you and I would no longer be held back by anything.

When we fail to see Jesus' sacrifice, we fail to feel His love. We mock Him as the soldiers did, and His death is minimized. Our past died on the cross that day, and our life rose again on the third day. Jesus didn't stay in the grave, nor did He simply forgive us of our sins. He made way for us to have an abundant life and an awakening for His mercies to be seen as new every morning.

God is always near. When you doubt His presence, look for it. Seek Him. He is close. He knows you, has heard your cries, and has wiped away all the tears of yesteryear. As Jeremiah 29:11 says, He knows the plan for your life because He has set it in motion and gives you a hope and a future. To God, you are like a flower in fertile soil that grows and becomes overwhelmingly, breathtakingly beautiful. That is you! Know that you are loved, and that God wants nothing more than for you to grow and flourish in every way He has promised you in His Word.

Too much time has passed. Don't waste one more day wondering why bad things have happened to you, why you lost when it certainly didn't seem fair, or why unforgiveness now resides in your heart. God did not intend that. He does not desire for you to live like a victim or be consumed by anger or pain until numbness overtakes your being. Open your hands. The day of ignoring is over. Today is the day that you lay it all down and pick up all the treasures God has promised. God's love is astounding. He wants you to recognize His face. He has placed joy in your spirit and hope in your heart. He is for you not against you. He delights in you!

Today is the day you release everything in your white-knuckled fists, place it all before Him, and walk away from it forever. The movement has begun; the mundane busyness is over, and life starts anew. The dream snatcher cannot squash your dreams, passions, or visions any longer.

Every movement requires commitment. A commitment to do just that—move. Now is the time for you to claim victory, to jump on the back of a white horse and ride to the next promise. No dream ever took place under your feet, so stop looking down. Death and fear are not allowed to take up residency for one more second in your life. It is time to move, look up, and rise to the challenge that God has called you. Today is the day you hear Him. It is time to claim your destiny and inheritance.

This is what I want you to do. Call out what holds you back and pull down the authority to change straight from heaven. Your part now, as silly as it may seem, is to speak the following words aloud. Call these things out over your life: "I am a beautiful, grace-filled, forgiven, child of God. Thank You, Father, that You intend everything good in my life. I lay down all that I have held too tightly and pick up all the love you have freely given. I am finished fighting alone, being alone, and moving alone. I want all of You and openly give You all of me. You are my Father, and I love you. Thank You for always being present in my life. Allow Your Spirit to fill all my empty places. May I gain ground and vision in this moment. Let Your movement flow through me and propel me with purpose and power into the place You have designed specifically for me. I will obediently follow where You lead. I will listen and not be afraid because I am Yours and You are mine. I know that You are on my side and trust that Your movement in my life will sweep me off my feet. I am ready, God. Help me to move."

Now claim it and believe it. It is time that you know you are worthy and to relinquish control and trust in the Father who will not let you down. It is not His character or nature to be anything less than perfect. He is ready to move. Unclench your fists, and allow His power and purpose to flow through you now.

4

Sitting Bird

Control isn't the only thing that holds us back from God's perfect plan. We can get so beaten up by life that eventually recoiling from it has no impact. We can be filled with such pain that life doesn't seem worth living. In those times, we fail to move altogether. Immobilization can cancel our dreams and power. The pain from our past can dictate our future choices. Do you feel scared or unable to move?

While driving one morning, I was deep in thought. There were no children in the car with me, so I was able to work through my day and simply get lost in the moment. It was one of those drives where I had no idea how I actually got to my destination. Everything is a blank, but God and autopilot got me safely where I needed to go.

I was on the highway and moving at a decent speed when, for some reason, my eye caught two black birds sitting in the adjacent lane up ahead. They didn't have much time to fly away. In my rearview mirror, I saw an eighteen-wheeler quickly approaching. Suddenly, one of the birds sprang to his feet and jumped up and down as if he was yelling at the other bird, "Get up, you silly bird! Look up! Something big is coming! You must move!"

The eighteen-wheeler passed me on the left. With less than a second before impact, the bird on his feet flew away while the other one became a pile of feathers. The bird was no match for the eighteen-wheeler. He was literally a sitting target.

I reenacted the scene in my mind. It was as if the one bird was urging the other to fly away, warning him that he was in immediate danger. But the other bird either chose to stay put or was unable to move.

We all have a choice to make when immobility sets in. We can remain exactly where we are, creating a life so busy and preoccupied that no one can get through to us. In this place, we become unavailable to others and their needs and can also lose the skills to move. Maybe we don't know any other way. This is survival mode, the eleventh inning, the end of the road, but we are still paralyzed. We can become paralyzed by fear of the unknown or that our abilities will not be good enough or by doubt. That bird was immobile for one reason or another. Maybe he was self-righteous and believed he was above harm. Whatever the reasons, the bird lost his life because he didn't move.

As I thought more about the birds, I realized that the one who flew away at the last minute also had a choice—to either die with his partner or get out of the way. The longer I thought about this, I recalled a story a few years earlier that impacted who I was as a mom and as a person.

We lived in a community with a pool. I had a two-year-old, a three-year-old, and was pregnant with my third child. At that point in my life, I really didn't know much about floatation devices; we simply went to the pool to enjoy the cool, refreshing water on a hot day.

One day, I dipped each boy in and swam him in circles while the other waited patiently. They were doing great, and we were having such fun, so we decided to play a game together. As I stood in the pool, the boys would jump in to me one at a time and would splash and then pretend to swim back to the side of the pool, where I lifted them back to safety. We continued this fun over and over. It was working; they were taking turns. No problem.

Then my three-year-old, Jacob, decided that walking to the other side of the pool would be a great idea. I held out my hand to my two-year-old, Levi, and told him to not jump in as I coaxed Jacob to rejoin the fun we were having only seconds before. He was no longer interested, but the even bigger problem was that he could not swim. Neither of the boys could swim.

Think … think … what should I do? I asked myself. My mind raced as I thought surely Levi would not jump. I was lost, confused, and literally in over my head. I wasn't certain I could move away from Levi and trust he wouldn't jump if I moved toward Jacob. No decision was a good one at this point. I wanted to scream, but I couldn't.

I took two steps toward Jacob when I heard the splash of two little boys who couldn't swim hit the water. Oh, God, what do I do? I have to go to the one closest to me, but then I can't save the other. How can I not save my child? Torment flooded my spirit as the water rushed over their heads. My body instinctively moved toward Levi since he was within reach. I scooped him out of the water, put him safely on dry ground, and felt my body go numb. The life inside me must have felt my anguish. I couldn't move. Exhaustion overcame my thoughts and my abilities.

A man who was sitting by the pool jumped in and brought

Jacob out of the water, gasping for air. All I could utter as I grabbed my child from him were, "Thank you." It was a mere whisper, at best. I moved with heavy legs to get to my children, embrace them, and quickly dry them and myself off for our return home.

Once I regained my senses, I looked where the man was sitting earlier, but he was no longer there. How would I find him? I needed to hug him. He had saved my child. That is no small task. He deserved a medal, a gift, or an award. But I could do nothing because he was gone.

When I couldn't move, when I was about to become a pile of feathers, God reminded me of His presence. I had never seen that man at the pool before, and I never saw him again. Maybe he was an angel sent for Jacob and me that day. Whoever he was, he moved with power and purpose. He didn't hesitate. He flew to the call that was placed before him and allowed himself to be the movement in that moment for someone he had never met. He looked up and listened. He could have been too busy or lost in his own world, but he wasn't. No, that man that day at the pool was in a movement.

I, however, was immobile. Although I meant well and clearly wanted to save my children, I was unable to. Despite my intentions, I absolutely could not move, and that inability haunted me. A few days later, I made a choice—the pool was off-limits. I conceded to the power of doubt and fear and allowed my circumstances to dictate my journey. I chose to become a victim.

I do understand that bad things happen to good people. Some of us have been victim to horrific events in our lives. Yet how we move out of those events or circumstances is our choice. We can either behave as a victim or claim our rightful destiny as a victor. I made the choice to be a victim that day at the pool and the days that followed. And it didn't last only a few days. It went on for months. My fear of the possibilities paralyzed me.

Eventually, my fear of the unknown was removed by the power of Christ, and I chose to move with purpose. My children deserved to go to the pool; they did not deserve to walk in worry, nor did they deserve to inherit the sins of their mother. I made the choice, if not for myself then for my children, to move. I then realized that God had provided a wonderful man that beautiful day, whether an angel or simply a human being in the right place at the right time, to save my son. The same son who would later remind me that I needed to see how much he loved me. I see it ... oh, how I see it. My child loves me, yet my Father loves me even more.

Our greatest choice, the most altering choice, is the one to move. We get to move in a way that is a powerful revolution of fearless love, and God can help us do that. We can urge someone along or pull them out of harm's way, or we can move simply because we need to get away. There are times in life when we become overwhelmed and overloaded, and the load is too much to carry. However, because of Jesus' love and sacrifice, we have the ability to experience a movement in spite of ourselves.

Our exhaustion, doubt, fear, and hurt took the form of three nails driven into a willing Savior. Jesus asked God if there was another way. He didn't desire for death to be His move, yet He was willing if that was His Father's will. He wanted to live, teach, and heal. His move looked different to Him than what God placed before Him. But Jesus' next move, fueled by forgiveness and love, was the perfect example of what power looks like in our lives. His movement was the embodiment of purpose, which was saving us.

God loves us in spite of ourselves. He may place before us a movement that seems too hard or even impossible, but we must accept it as Jesus did in faith and love for Him. We cannot become victim to fear and doubt. We cannot sit, unwilling to move. God wants us to throw away our busyness and pour our affection onto Him.

Being immobile is a move of sorts. It, too, comes with choice. We choose to not have time for others, to live in fear, frustration, and staleness. Without movement in the sea of life, algae grow and take over until, eventually, we get lost. That is not God's plan for our lives. When we don't move, we are choosing to die. So right here in this moment, I compel you to move.

Maybe that means beginning with a prayer for God to show you what your next step should be. Maybe it is writing all your dreams down on paper and why they have or have not come to pass. Maybe it is starting with a phone call of forgiveness. Maybe it is recognizing the sin that has taken up residency in your life. Don't be afraid. With movement comes risk, but moving is an act of obedience to God, who has called you to something more. You wouldn't willingly lay in front of an eighteen-wheeler or jump in a pool and not swim or sit still as a roaring fire moved closer. But that is what you are doing when you don't move; whatever the reason, you are suffocating and your heart is stopping. You have forgotten who you are and who you were created to be.

Jesus was obedient to His Father no matter what lay ahead, even if it was not the plan He saw for Himself. Jesus' life was a powerful, purposeful movement that is ours to embrace as the perfect example.

Jesus was a superhero, the conqueror of the world, yet He never fought on any battlefield. He bears the scars of a hero on

His hands, feet, and side. To not move is to challenge His very existence. He wants every good thing for you and every dream He has placed in your heart to come to life. You must look up, rise up, and move.

5

Bring On the Power and the Roadkill

To be part of God's movement is to feel His life-changing power pulsing through your body. Then you can love and live with purpose as you have never loved or lived before. It is the time to move forward. Faith lies in the unknown.

God tells us that faith the size of a mustard seed can move a mountain. That we can tell the mountain to jump into the sea and it will jump. Now that is power! Our faith moves us from past to purpose. We are not held captive but rather are champions. If you have ever been to a sporting event, you have probably heard the song "We are the Champions." That could be our theme as followers of Christ. We are privileged to be part of the movement He is working through us, and we are champions because we are His.

James 2:17 tells us, "In the same way, faith by itself, if it is not accompanied by action is dead." If we are not actively seeking God's purpose for our lives, we have ceased to live. The movement of God is active and alive. With power and purpose, He thrusts us into His divine light to build our character. The self-loathing and pity party is over. God's heart is not for you to bear the sins of your past. He sent His Son to bear them on your behalf. You may have done things you are not proud of and have been something to someone else that God never intended for you. You may have hurt others so deeply that their wounds are still raw. Or maybe the scars are something you bear. Whatever has happened should not dictate what can happen. You are His creation, and He wants you to walk in a mountain-moving, unhindered faith. His plan is for you to move with such confidence that nothing or no one can stand in your way—not even you. So often we are own biggest enemy.

There is great risk in having such purpose. It's scary to fail. Yet the greatest failure is where no risk is taken. How can you succeed if you never take action? As James 2 tells us, our faith must have action, for it shows the power of God that exists in us when we know Him as our Savior.

A movement of God is not running away from something or someone but rather running to something or someone. When God surrounds us with His goodness, the toxicity that has held us back is no longer in control. Faith takes over and power rises. The mountain is moving, friends. Yes, it is moving. Let your faith rise, and get ready to say, "Jump!"

A mountain moved in my very own yard one hot spring afternoon. While playing outside, my animal-loving boys found a dead bunny in the street, or more precisely, roadkill—a flat, deader than dead, smashed little bunny. You see, we had a bunny that lived in our yard. We left him carrots to snack on and watched him hop around our home, nibbling the grass. The bunny was our pet, of sorts. You know, the kind you can't touch, but you watch and claim them with some sense of ownership. Having this preexisting relationship, the sight of this lifeless creature rocked my children to their core. They were heartbroken, so our next step was to give the little gray fellow a proper burial.

Two of my children dug the hole where we laid his lifeless body, and the other two stood by, watching and absorbing. My youngest boys, Gavin and Asher, needed to say a few words before we could lay him to rest. The eulogies went something like this, "He was a good bunny," "I am sure his mom will miss him because I sure will," "Oh, little sweet bunny, sleep well," etc.

As their condolences came to an end, something clicked. Asher exclaimed, "We need to pray over this bunny! He can be healed! How about this? After we bury him, we will pray, and—poof —God will just heal him!"

Jacob, my logical oldest child, said, "Yeah, like Lazarus? Not going to happen! The guy barely has a head!" I was secretly laughing but let this play out.

We placed the bunny in the hole, gently covered him up, and prayed for him as we stood over the loose pile of dirt. My older boys were already at peace. However, Asher, decided to share, "God, we will miss this bunny. But take good care of him in heaven, and we will see him again someday!" Then, as if time stood still, he started digging up our burial site.

I immediately stopped him.

He looked at me, frustrated. "Mom, why can't I dig? The bunny will be gone because he is hopping around in heaven with Jesus now!"

Wow, I was in awe of my child's faith. I then understood Luke 18:16, "But Jesus called the children to him and said, 'Let the little children come to me, and do not hinder them, for the kingdom of God belongs to such as these.'" The kingdom of

God belongs to the children, or those who believe with such purity and faith that a deceased bunny is no longer lifeless.

Psalm 116:6 says, "The Lord protects those of childlike faith." Asher's faith was larger than mine ever was. He believed in healing, in the very Spirit of God to breathe life back into a bunny that barely had a head. His faith believed that God did not deem any life as less important than another. While he was believing for miracles and greatness, my mind was trapped, only picturing the moment I could take my children in and wash death off their hands.

Yes, my child showed me that day how real God was in his life. Was He that real in mine? Asher didn't blink an eye at the power of God. He didn't hesitate for a moment to believe that God could heal or be that present in what seemed irrelevant to me. Tears filled my eyes when I realized my feeble-mindedness. I desperately wanted Asher's kind of faith to indwell my soul.

Smiling, I looked up to the skies as if I could see the face of Jesus, and sent my children inside to wash their hands. I had a crazy thought, but I knew that if I didn't go, I would be bound by the things of this world and the chains that were already too binding.

I snuck back to that freshly covered burial site and dug, wondering if it would really be empty as my child had said. I thought about the "what ifs." I burrowed deeper, and then my dirt-covered hands and packed fingernails hit it. The bunny was still there. Still deader than dead, lifeless, in the same hole where we had left him. I have to admit I was a little bummed, thinking God was going to do something so cool, more amazing than anything my child had ever seen or experienced. He would then glorify God, telling all his friends and shouting it in all places, unashamed. Why hadn't God raised this little bunny? He surely could have. He was more than capable.

Then I got it as I threw loose soil back over the miniature Peter Cottontail. It was never about my four-year-old. He didn't need to see a resurrected body. He believed it was possible, and because of that, it became a reality in his life. He believed that God was bigger than anything he could ever imagine, and that God was on his side. And he knew that God wanted everything great for his life, even the bunny's life. Asher believed that mountains could be moved.

No, that day was for me. God showed me what faith looked like through my child's eyes. It was big and strong and good and, boy, was it powerful. God wanted me to move. He wanted me to believe the same thing my child believed that day. That God could raise that bunny because He is present and powerful, which is tough to see sometimes. Even though the bunny was still there, I walked out with a childlike faith and dug and pursued the power of a Savior.

Sometimes we feel like roadkill. Left on the side of the road with only a faint pulse, barely alive. We feel left behind by those who have run us over and in turn become lifeless. Yet in the distance we see a light. The feeble breath we take isn't enough to muster up a word of help, but the light draws closer, and hope is clearer. Our Savior has come to lift us from the ashes and bring us into the beauty promised through His death on a cross. When we see the beauty of what once was motionless and mirrored death, we know that our future rests in His hands. We must take a stand and no longer live seeing only the finite things of this earth, those things that will fade away and be no more. Life can feel heavy and spiritless when we only see though human eyes.

When we view life solely in the physical, we worry. We become concerned about the way others see us. Many of us have had poor self-esteem at one point or another. Maybe it was because we didn't look like someone else or our clothes weren't new or our checking account balance wasn't large or our children weren't well-behaved. One thing is for certain: We can busy ourselves with too much care about what others think. God didn't design us to worry about such things. Many times we see ourselves as we were never intended to. The Enemy attacks us with those lies and alters the way we think God sees us.

The question should be, how do we see ourselves through the presence of God living through us? When God breathes into us, we have been made righteous, and we are to see ourselves through the life-giving presence of Jesus. He is faithful. He will take our sinful nature and transform it into new light through the holy nature of our Father. We are a metamorphosis in the making. Change takes place as God sends a movement to transform our lives to impeccable beauty.

We have friends who had an amazing caterpillar garden. Dozens of those creatures moved around in this garden, eating and growing, until they were ready to take the next step in their journey of life.

The neatest thing about caterpillars is the time before they form their chrysalis. When the caterpillars stop growing, they prepare for the next stage of their being. They move to a high place, some as high as they can possibly go, and begin forming a structure around their body. Then the most spectacular transformation happens, turning the ordinary caterpillar into a completely different yet beautiful creation, the butterfly, from a combination of hard work, waiting for God to move, and then breaking free from the chrysalis to begin its journey toward all that it was designed to be. The butterfly is born out of life that already existed but was not yet completed as God planned.

That is a representation of our lives. Whether by choices we have made or choices inflicted upon us, we get to be part of a movement that erases the old creature and transforms us into the one God intended. God is the only one who can birth new life in us. He gives us the strength to break free from the chains that hold us back and expand our wings to fly to a new destination—a place where we decide to not be concerned with how others see us, to not be bothered by what once was, or be bound to a world that attempts to tell us we aren't enough. Once the chains are broken, we begin focusing on the only One who matters and the truth of His love. He will birth new revelations in our spirit. Ask for it; no tricks or clever words are needed. Only a heart willing to walk out an unhindered faith.

God will give you fresh revelation when you ask Him. He wants you to see things from His perspective and is always willing to give them to you. God works through those things that speak to our lives. Because I enjoy a good punch line, God spoke to me in such a way I could understand.

Many years ago when I was in college, I met Ashley, an amazing guy. However, while most of the girls I knew attended college for their MRS degree, I was looking to get my undergraduate degree and then go on for my PhD. I had a plan, and nothing was going to stop me. Well, nothing except God. My plan was not God's plan. Ashley pursued me with intention and gentleness, something I had never known. But I was not interested because I had years of schooling ahead of me and didn't want anything to get in my way. But the more I ran, the more restless I became. I did not understand what God was doing. Shouldn't He have been proud of me for focusing on my education with such vigor? I wrestled with God and wondered why I did not have peace.

One evening I was sitting in my car at the train tracks behind our college campus. The gates were down, as there was an oncoming train. Desperate, I decided to use that time to talk to God, so I asked Him for a sign. I am not sure if that was something I had ever done before. I wasn't sure how I felt about throwing out the fleece to God. Yet that night I needed a sign. I rested my hands on the steering wheel, waiting for the train to pass, and told God I needed to know right then if I was to choose Ashley. If I did, I knew it didn't mean I couldn't still focus on school, but I knew things would change. Was Ashley the plan God had for my life?

Immediately, an Ashley furniture train car passed by. What was a moment before a distress call to my Savior turned into laughter as God spoke to me about my next step. He gave me revelation because I asked and earnestly sought Him. How cool God is, I thought. The movement began, and Ashley and I started dating. The walls around me began coming down. My life was not playing out as I had imagined. It was much better.

Ashley and I were married two and half years later. We have been married over eighteen years now, and he has never disrespected or dishonored the sanctity of our marriage. He is and has been my best friend, my heart, and my life and is an amazing father—all the things I did not have. God's revelation that lonely night at the train tracks continues to bless my life and bring me incredible joy today and hopefully many more to come.

Yes, God is always ready to give new revelations. He wants us to want His plan. His desire is that we would seek Him with such passion that our longing is to hear the heart of our Father. We have the privilege to see God's plan. But the choice to ask is ours. Even more so is our choice to listen and move as He directs. Ask God now for His revelation and for His plan to be released in your life and faithfully walk out the story He has written specifically for you.

Maybe this is the moment God stirs up a vision, a dream, or a movement that you had placed aside. Maybe you did so because you didn't believe in yourself, thought others would think you were crazy, or feared rejection. Jesus lived this day after day, but the difference with Him is that He lived out the life created for Him by His Father and left all the rejection, crazy talk, and worry in God's hands. When we live sold out for Jesus, we focus less upon what others think and run full out after the heart of God. We care more about the opportunities we are privileged to have aching and burning inside of us, ready to be used for His glory. When we mark a movement happening within us, we walk out in an unstoppable faith. Nothing can stand in its way.

One of the most beautiful passages of Scripture is Luke 8 where we find Jesus walking through a crowd. Not just any crowd, but one that was so tight and busy it almost crushed Him. This crowd could have prevented movement. It could have forced someone to give up due to obstacles that were too large to hurdle. People were crammed together, shoulder to shoulder, side to side.

Despite the crowd, a woman moved through it with purpose and power. Though her body was frail, she refused to give up. She had suffered from a bleeding issue for several years, and although she was weak from blood loss, she was determined to work her way through the masses. She was faithful and unwilling to surrender to the disease in her body or to the crowd that stood in her way. The words I quit did not exist in her vocabulary. The woman had purpose behind her movement and knew that Jesus was the source of her healing.

As she drew closer, she reached out and her fingers brushed the hem of Jesus' garment. The Bible uses the word cloak, meaning a coat or something loose. The woman knew in her heart that simply touching the hem of Jesus' garment would heal her body. When she did so, her bleeding stopped, and she was immediately healed. Imagine twelve years of nonstop bleeding and in an instant it is gone because you moved with purpose!

The remainder of the story in Luke 8:45-48 NLT reads as follows: "Who touched me?" Jesus asked. Everyone denied it, and Peter said, "Master, this whole crowd is pressing up against you." But Jesus said, "Someone deliberately touched me, for I felt healing power go out from me." When the woman realized that she could not stay hidden, she began to tremble and fell to her knees in front of him. The whole crowd heard her explain why she had touched him and that she had been immediately healed. "Daughter," he said to her, "your faith has made you well. Go in peace."

Wow! How incredible! The woman pressed through the crowd, refused to give up, and moved with such intentional, faithful purpose that she was healed in an instant. God gave her all that she sought. Her faith led her to move. She wasn't too busy; she wasn't trying it out just to see if it worked. She left her home that day to touch Jesus, even if only His coat, because she knew that would bring her life. She didn't care what others thought or that it seemed impossible. The woman believed that Jesus would heal her and nothing stopped her from getting to Him. She was not afraid to move with purpose. That is a movement of God.

6

Paper Jesus

It had been a long day, and patience was wearing thin, including mine. My boys and I were on our way home and couldn't wait to get there. So like all tired, giddy, and crazed children, they began singing a medley of songs. They were raising the roof and letting the dogs out and rocking out the bones that were almost too tired to move. Then they threw their arms up and chanted, "Everybody who loves Jesus raise your hands in the air!" Nothing earth-shattering or mind-blowing, certainly not lyrics any record label would be picking up, but they were occupied, content, and moving at the same time. I drove, drowning in my thoughts, as my children chanted the same ten words over and over. It could have been worse. At least Jesus was being glorified.

Then it began. The fight over what would go down in history as one of the silliest arguments I have ever witnessed. My mind was numb, and my ability to remain alert was fading fast. As I drifted into my own little world, the voices in the back grew louder and louder. Two of my children sitting in the third row began fighting over a piece of paper. It wasn't cool. It wasn't colorful. It was a small, lifeless piece of paper. "No, it's mine" bounced back and forth like a tennis ball on the courts of Wimbledon. The two in the middle seat looked back, wondering if this was something worth their energy. If it was good enough, it could be anyone's game. The cycle was relentless, and no one was willing to surrender. It was absolutely ridiculous.

The little strength I had left was only enough to round up a simple "Stop." But it did nothing. It was as if my mouth had never moved. Sensing my fatigue, one of my children sitting in the middle row looked back at his brothers and said, "Please, boys. It's just a piece of paper. I mean, with all this commotion, you would think it was a paper Jesus. Is it a paper Jesus? No. So you shouldn't want anything but Jesus that bad!"

Everyone stopped squabbling, and the car grew silent. My son reminded his brothers that life can get out of hand, even become ridiculous, if we allow it. He explained to them in a childlike way that all the foolishness is simply that, foolish. Focusing on the mundane, the next busy task, or the pursuit of the flesh when instead we should see Jesus in His deity. We can so easily fight over what is useless instead of exploring the greatness of God. When we see Jesus for who He is and what He has done for us, we should only want Him with such passion. The things of this world should be cast away so we can grasp the love only He can offer. Our heartbeat then acts as an extension of His.

If we know that to be true, why do we choose immobilization or fear? Maybe it is easier, less painful. Maybe because we are so stuck in our routine that we can't see our way out. Perhaps your life has a rhythm; it runs the way you like without too many bumps and doesn't require much thought. Yet my question to you would be, what kind of music are you producing? Is the rhythm in sync? Is it smooth and effortless? My guess is no. Just as a bad song is to our ears, so is a life out of rhythm to the heart of God. He meant good for you; otherwise, He wouldn't have offered the gift of His Son. You may not think you are worth it, and by human standards, none of us are worth it. Yet He extended His hand. Grace reached out to pull us in. You are worth it. He made that possible. No matter the mistakes you made, the burdens you carry, or the heaviness you bear, you are worth it! The nail-scarred hands are the evidence.

Thinking that the God of the universe has time to comfort you and call you into your place of righteousness can be difficult. God is holy and sees you by way of the cross. However, the miracle of the cross and His redeeming grace is that He can bring us, the unholy, into the very standard of Himself, the Holy One. God's holy love brings us to who we were created to be. In 1 John 4:8, we read, "God is love," whereas in John 3:16, we see that love in action as God sent His Son as a sacrifice for the world. Love came down from heaven and gave us life. God didn't love us because we were lovable. It is His nature to love us because He is love. Clinging to the truth in 1 John 4:8, how could we ever think we are not enough for God? He is love; therefore, He is not driven by emotion or actions. Scripture does not say He loves us when we do good deeds or work harder than anyone else. No, it simply says that God is love, and that that love is directed to you and me. We are His purpose. Through that love, He wants to push us into the movement He has composed as a beautiful orchestra conducted with harmony.

You are brought into God's standard. This is a faith walk, a place where God matures us day after day. We must try with everything in us to keep moving, not give up, and press into all that God has to offer. He is breathing newness and an awakening into your life. There is something you have to put down that you will pick back up. There is something you didn't even know was present, but God is revealing it to you now. God is speaking in this moment and moving you in a healthy way. You have a calling on your life. The question is, will you walk through the remaining years of your life only to be in the same place at the end? I am certain that is not your desire.

So my hope and unending prayer is that this book will reignite a fire in you, and that God will give you everything you need. The choice to begin a movement in your life is yours. Remember, anything you are meant to do is not too small or too big. You are meant to change lives. Jesus changed lives one person at a time. Most of us are called to make a difference on the road we walk. Let's face it; many of us will not speak on a massive stage or have our thoughts publicized. No, our road, the beautiful road laid out specifically for us, will touch many lives through our daily encounters that God places before us. Pray for divine interactions each day, and stand ready for God to give them to you. We can open our ears to what God has to say, open our mouths to speak only what He has us to speak, open our hearts so He can lead us, and open our lives to follow Him no matter where He might take us. Remember, this life is a journey. One that is made with power and meant for purpose.

Believe that the God of the universe—the One who put spots on the ladybug and a tuxedo on the penguin, who gave us redwood trees and pine cones, the sea horse and the blue whale—created you. He set in motion a purpose, a plan, and a destiny for your life. He created no other creature with such love as He did you. His plan and purpose is yours. He will give you mountain peaks instead of valleys if only you ask. He is ready. He wants to move in ways that are mind-blowing, jaw-dropping, awe-inspiring, and life-giving. He wants to breathe newness into and bear life where thorns have grown.

God is ready to set forth a movement in you that cannot be stopped or altered. You are redeemed, and you are His capable child. Your destiny has been born; the movement is set. It is your time. God has released power and authority into your life and spirit. Be ready because the wave of awakening will flood your soul and move you into waters deeper than you ever imagined. You have been in the shallow water for far too long.

When you move into deeper waters, you will move closer to God and His calling. In the deep there will be more risks. Sharks may threaten to eat your dreams and other creatures may prey on your weaknesses, but you must keep moving. The Enemy is always scheming to squash dreams and desires. When you sit still fewer threats circle you because you are doing less for the Kingdom and are no threat to the Enemy because you are stagnant. But God is present and will not allow the Enemy to gain control. Remember, the battle has already been won, and Satan only has as much power as you give him.

Be clear, however, that being still does not always mean that you are stagnant. God can also be active in the stillness of rest, which is different from being immobilized by an emotion evoked by the Enemy. God works through us when we seek Him, and we can actively pursue Him through our quiet, intimate times by praying and reading His Word. Even though it may seem at times that nothing is moving or we can't press on, there is something happening in the spiritual realm. This is the time when the Holy Spirit is the most active, fighting for you and speaking on your behalf. This is a time to listen and rest, as your body is being refueled for what is coming next. Being still in God simply means that you are actively seeking

His will and plan for your life as you listen for His voice. Rest in Him, and allow His presence to wash over you. Things will begin to make sense and come into focus. Once the movement has become clear in the spiritual, it is our responsibility to move in the physical.

Oftentimes, we are too busy to stop and listen or we don't want to be bothered with any other purpose than our own. We can feel overwhelmed and overrun by our circumstances. Maybe we don't want to listen because we have given up and are angry with life and even with God. It is easy to look at someone else and wonder why their life seems calm when ours feels like chaos squared. Feeling sorry for ourselves will get us nowhere fast.

If you are exhausted, beat up, and ready to give up, right now in this moment drop to your knees, throw your hands in the air, and call out to your Savior. He is there, always has been, and is ready to heal your hurt and put His loving arms around you. Wipe away the negative thoughts, doubt, and pain and move toward Him, hands out, ready to walk in faith with your Father. As long as you follow God, your movement will always be forward. His unconditional, selfless love will stand the test of time. It is a love that no power can pierce and no bully can alter.

God is not small or simple. He has a mind-blowing, outrageous imagination. In His wild, crazy way, He is urging you to follow Him. You can move one way or the other. You will either keep pressing on toward all that God has called you to or you will turn away and bear the weight and shame for a lifetime. Maybe you have already chosen your path; it can't be changed, you can't go back. What's done is done. If so and you feel ashamed or guilty, remember it has been covered. Often when we make irreversible decisions all we can depend on is an all-forgiving God.

We have each made decisions we regret. Yet those moments mark our lives for change. This journey of life is not meant merely for surviving but for living out the fullness of God and believing in His grace. Do you think the Father's love is dependent upon any choice you make, whether good or not so good? Absolutely not. His love is not limited or conditional. Remember, God is love. So when we make a choice that may not align with His heart, we must repent, go back to Him, and seek His plan the next time. We will make mistakes, but returning to Him is where healing begins. It is there where He points us back to His Word that encompasses all the promises He has spoken into existence.

When we fail to seek Him and depend on our own devices, we become exhausted and stuck, feel stranded and abandoned, and then get lost in a dry and weary land. We will remain there until everything shifts and we see the oasis indicating that hope lies ahead. Hope is to desire something with confident expectation of its fulfillment, and to live with confident expectation is hope alive. Did you catch that? Living with unhindered faith and the expectation of the fulfillment of God's promises is a living, breathing hope within each of us.

If we lose hope, everything we know becomes wrong. Our vision blurs, our mouth becomes dry, our heart races, and our perspective is completely altered. We wander through the desert unable to find security and fulfillment. We can thirst for and dream about it, but if we take our eyes off what lays ahead even for a second our journey can shift. Satan wants nothing more than to keep us dry and weary, to live without hope. But Jesus in His very essence is hope. And His hope is that our faith will not waiver in the power of God's love and the grace offered through nail-scarred hands. We have life and, it is promised, in abundance.

The Enemy's goal is for us to lack confidence in God. He wants to steal our joy and rob us of our destiny. But he can only do so if we choose to stay in the desert. However, when we choose to run full out toward the affection of our Father, He quenches every thirst, holds our hand, puts His gentle arm around us, and walks us to safety.

Life can be a dry place at times or Life can be dry at times. Yet no matter what is thrown your way, remind yourself that the God of the universe created you. He has a calling on your life, and it does not include the desert. Change your perspective. Set your eyes on God's grace. Expecting fulfillment will lead to the understanding that God's favor lasts a lifetime. When you believe that grace is freely given, the scales will fall from your eyes and your vision will become clear. Focus on today, right now; the journey ahead will come into view. Once your vision is unclouded, you can live freely in the hope and grace of the Savior.

Walking in His love may not take away all the heaviness, but it will certainly lighten the load. Growth and newness will flow through the movement of God, leading you to the oasis. The Water of Life bears fruit because nourishment comes from Him. If you stay oppressed by your past or mistakes, you will remain in the desert, and you certainly cannot bear fruit there. God has promises over you and is not finished with you. So do not lose hope. I once heard a saying about hope that has stayed with me. "You can live weeks without food, days without water, minutes without air, but you can't live a second without hope."

Don't live with regrets. So what if it didn't work out exactly as you imagined? The greatest ache is less about whether something worked or not, but whether you tried to see if it was even possible. When you lay your head on your pillow at night, will you be more concerned that something didn't go as planned or that you didn't even give it a shot? Let go of those things that define you today for what you did in your past. Let go of those people you have allowed to determine your direction because you gave them that power. Let go of all the things that hold you back. Jesus walked fearlessly before the people who doubted His authority and did not acknowledge the cynics who tried to smother His goodness. Jesus lived as the person His Father created Him to be. He was not embarrassed, nor did he allow others to dictate, determine, or define His future. He knew that only God had that power.

I have worked through some difficult things in my life. There have been times when things were so awful and impossible that I wondered why I had to endure such heartache. Yet even though I couldn't see it at the time, those experiences held much promise and purpose. Those tough places made me stronger, wiser, and bolder and deepened my faith in God and His outrageous imagination.

Through some of those tough places, though, I allowed fear and thoughts of failure to rest on me. Years ago, I took a survey on the fear of failure. My results were off the chart. They indicated that experiences of failure dominated my memory, and that my problems in this area would remain until I took some definitive action. Well, many years later, I did just that. From the time I was a teenager, I felt in my heart that I was supposed to write, but that seemed too big and scary. I was afraid to write because I feared others rejecting it. Then one day while talking to God, He told me to squash the negative self-talk along with the fear and let the Enemy know that he no longer had authority over my life. I asked God to breathe into me the very words He wanted to speak through me. I realized that even if I was writing for only one other person that was enough.

So I followed God, believing in His plan for my life, and

understood for the first time the fullness of my Father and how He wanted everything good for me. My stepping out in faith and obedience was what He was looking for. And it is the same for you. God simply wants you to throw off all the junk that holds you back. He wants to bring you into a new life with Him. He wants you to step out in faith and walk.

When your child takes a step for the first time, you wouldn't dream of pushing him down or holding him back. You would undoubtedly grab every recording device you could find and begin taping, for you would want to capture every moment. Maybe you would share it with the grandparents. Maybe you would show your friends. Maybe you would save it for him someday to remind him that at some point he will have to take the risk again and trust that he can actually take that first step. For all of us, once we take the first step and realize we can do it, we take the next. Yes, we might fall. We might get bruised and hurt along the way. But none of that matters because we are moving.

You have found a new freedom. You are now able to stand tall and make a movement happen. Once you have taken steps three, four, and five, steps six, seven, and eight become easier. Freedom is found in moving. Be part of a movement with purpose that brings you into that freedom. Once you gain your balance and strength, you will be able to bring others on the journey with you. You can encourage them through your example of faith.

Your first steps can happen today. Step out without fear and move with the purpose of becoming free from the chains that have held you back. Break free from the bondage; allow it to own you no longer. This is your day of freedom and seeing the greatness of God. His hope and grace are yours; choose to receive them and move in His promise. Reach out to Him. Want Jesus that bad.

7

The "I's" Have It

Each day offers many possibilities that are yours for the taking. You have been given gifts, talents, and abilities that are ready to be unleashed and have a power within you that is ready to come alive that offers greatness and has unmatched authority.

This authority develops your character so you may actively give to others—to care, share, and help when others are in need. It is your duty as a follower of Christ to invest in others. Then when you feel bankrupt, those friends who have been ordained specifically for your life will fill you up. Make it your goal to have a handful of close friends, as this keeps you mindful of others. You should also have at least one friend older than you who can mentor you. Maybe someone with more life experience than you. This may be something you need to ask for. If you do not have these relationships currently in your life, I urge you to find them. This is an important part in the journey of movement.

Jesus gave us that example through His relationship with His disciples. He chose those men to be a part of His life, not because they were popular or because He thought they would make Him look better. No, the Bible says that Jesus spent an entire night praying about whom He would choose to stand beside Him and be there for Him. Those men were not perfect, but they were the men God led Jesus to choose.

We are reminded of the disciples' humanness in the midst of Jesus' holiness. Sometimes they let Him down. They didn't always come through. But for the most part, they loved Him and would do anything for His movement. His heart was for their success, and he displayed his gentle love for them and humility by washing their feet. This was a symbol of His love—a holy God in the form of a man cleaning dirt-stained, weathered feet. His Father was continually guiding and directing Him. God never left His side and constantly reminded Jesus of His love and all that He was capable of conquering.

I haven't always had those relationships in my life, but I am so blessed today to say that I do. I have one friend who is an absolute spiritual ambassador. When I pray for her, I find she has been on her knees before the throne of Jesus on my behalf. I have another friend who I know is there for me come rain or shine. She is a rock in my life. Another friend makes me laugh. I could be going through a terrible time and may begin crying to her, but I end up laughing with her. And then there is my encourager. She always lifts me up, even when I think I am lifting her up, and I feel better just being in her presence. And another friend I have is one I know I can trust with every desire of my heart. She keeps that sacred between us and spurs me on in my quest of our Savior.

It's funny how God brings the right people into our lives at the perfect time. Some relationships may last for years, and some may last a lifetime. Whatever the situation, usually those people we pour ourselves into become the pourers, the people who lift us up when the weight of life bogs us down. They offer exactly what we need, and prayerfully, we give back even more. Then we realize we are blessed with an earthly accountability. We have authority to speak life because God walks before us. Others recognize His love in us and want that love. When we adhere to the nature of Christ, others will be drawn to walk with Him.

There are four "I's" in the journey of movement, qualities Jesus expressed in who He was and is. These qualities likewise promote health in our souls, hearts, and minds. However, it is our choice to cling to and claim them as our own or not. We are created in His image. If these are God's qualities, we should want them as well.

The first "I" is integrity. Integrity is vital and includes honesty, a good reputation, and character that does not give in to temptation. Integrity is the secret place in our lives where the cobwebs reside, what we are when no one is looking. Integrity shines light on those secret things, and they come boldly out of hiding. Whole and true, integrity is the foundation for what follows.

I remember a time when I dialed a friend. This would normally have been a good thing—a time to catch up, chat, and listen. The problem was, I didn't know I called her. You know, one of those pocket dials. I had two boys in the bath, and we had to be somewhere in ten minutes. I procrastinated getting them out as I busied myself rounding up supplies for our trip. Finally, I laid out a towel and stressed the importance of their getting out now, as there was no time to waste.

But the water must have been thick in their ears because they certainly were not listening. The third time I told them, the phone somehow dialed the number to my friend, who heard me—not my finest hour. As the boys had yet to move, I yelled,

"Get out of the tub, and I won't tell you again!" Finally, after four times and a much-elevated blood pressure, they emerged from the bubble-filled tub to dry off.

Then I looked down. What? My phone was on with my friend's name at the top! I brought the phone to my ear, thinking maybe she wasn't there. But, oh, how wrong I was. When I heard her hello, I went mute. How awful I must have sounded to her as I yelled at my children. She didn't know I had asked them three times prior. But did that matter? I was so embarrassed that I couldn't speak and hit the "end call" button. My friend had heard me in my secret place, which she didn't need to hear. My voice was irritated and ugly.

I had a choice to make in that moment. I thought and thought, and the only obvious conclusion was to lie. So I called her again, this time knowingly, and acted as if something tragic had happened, and that I had to raise my voice to prevent injury. But this was not true. The only injury at this point was what I was doing to my insides. Lying wasn't something I normally did and definitely not well. Actually, I detest it, from my lips or anyone else's. But in that moment, I lied. I was sad that my friend heard my frustration, how my voice grew louder and more abrasive the more irritated I became. My friend rarely saw me frazzled. She thought I was calm and collected. Wow, she got an awakening that day! Would I ever look the same to her? I fussed over this and finally prayed, asking for forgiveness. God simply said, "Let it go."

But that was hard for me; all I wanted to do was bring it up and make it right. My friend would have forgiven me and shown great mercy, so I couldn't understand why God wouldn't allow me to correct what I had done. However, God reminded me that I am not perfect and should not pretend to be so. I then made a choice. While being a woman of integrity, I could still be real. We too often put on a beautiful façade, masking the dirt and grime beneath. No matter the circumstance, we are human. We will mess up. We will make mistakes. But our imperfection does not define who we are in our humanness.

I am still all that God created me to be. While lying and getting upset certainly wasn't right, I will try hard to not let it happen again. I didn't want my friend to lose trust in me or think I was a loose cannon, but wasn't that obvious in my actions? I did not want to hurt anyone or be hurt.

God is forgiving, and that day, more than anything, I had to forgive myself. It was a lesson in humility. It was also a lesson that integrity cannot be lost in a sentence. It can certainly be altered but isn't who we are. We are flawed people on a quest toward greatness to show others the unwavering love of Jesus. He showed me that day that people are more flexible than I thought. There was no excuse for my mistake, I couldn't erase it, but I could rewrite the next chapter with more love, character, and integrity to gain the hearts of those around me.

Yes, integrity is important, as it shows our devotion and proves our love for Jesus. When integrity resides within us, we move freely through the next "I's" and allow them to blossom in our souls.

The next "I" is the tricky one. So often we walk through our day-to-day routine like robots. We get locked into a system and don't want to detour from the plan we have set in motion. Oftentimes, as the morning fades into the evening, we have lost all sense of time, the bigger picture, and ourselves as routine takes over. Who are we? Have we lost the ability to even know? No, we have not. Maybe the skill set to be able to start. Or the desire. But we have the power to change our course and see the beautiful new life that only God can give.

The next "I" is identity. We have allowed what was to define what is or is yet to come. When our rose-colored glasses turn black, we lose our way. Throw off the glasses, and look to who you were created to be. You were certainly not created to be a victim, a martyr, or anything less than what has been promised. You are not your past. You are not the sins others have inflicted upon you, nor are you the sins you have wrapped yourself up in to numb the pain. You are a blood-bought, grace-given, mercy-holding, love-breathing child of God. You may have endured hard things, but you are not those things. You are a victor through the sacrifice and love of Jesus. Even when giving His life for us, Christ allowed a criminal to walk into His kingdom simply because he asked. The criminal sought Jesus, knowing He was greater than death. He believed in Jesus, walked in faith, and knew that his past actions didn't dictate his importance to the Savior. The criminal asked, and he received.

The criminal is a great example to us who get lost in our identity. The word identity is, simply stated, who one is. Here is the thing: If we are created in the image of God, how can we doubt the fact of who we are? No matter our circumstances or where we have been, God still defines us as His child. We are children of a King, and not just any king—the King. Jesus never doubted His identity. He knew who He was and understood His purpose.

Jesus also believed in the integrity and identity of His followers. Peter, for instance, denied Jesus three times, just as Jesus predicted. Peter was impulsive and made poor decisions at times. Yet Jesus loved Peter and saw his worth. He also knew Peter's faults but trusted his heart more. Even though Peter made mistakes, as all of us will, his integrity went before him and his identity was found in Jesus, not in his faults. Jesus believed in Peter so much that in Matthew 16:18, Jesus says, "And I tell you, that you are Peter, and on this rock, I will build my church, and all the powers of hell will not conquer it." God took a foolish man and turned him into the rock upon which Jesus built His church. So despite your faults, God stands ready to make a miracle out of you—one that can only come from the love of the Father.

God has used and still uses ordinary people to do extraordinary things. Look at the people Jesus chose to walk with Him throughout His life. He allows those of us who may never be famous to touch lives in ways we never imagined. Think about it. Peter was a regular guy who God transformed into a rock to build His church upon. God used fishermen, shepherds, and a woman at a well. It is amazing what ordinary people can do when they trust and follow an extraordinary God. Wrap your identity up in Him, what He is doing in your life, and what He is yet to do.

When we allow the naysayers and doubters to flood our thoughts, we get distracted. This is the Enemy's tool to hold us in bondage. When we give him permission to fill us with negative self-talk, we give him power that was never intended, like a puppeteer controlling our thoughts and movements. God didn't create us to be under anyone's control. He created us to be in His care, to walk in faith that moves through a crowd to touch the hem of His garment and can move mountains. That is not possible as long as we are in bondage or believe the lies that we are less than and simply not good enough. If we bow to that power, we lose our freedom.

Freedom is ours, and our identity is found in that freedom. It is what Jesus did for us on the cross. It is our covering. But like the criminal who hung beside our Savior, we have a choice to make: to allow the lies of the Enemy to bombard and immobilize us or to rise above our circumstances and claim victory. God intends us to live lives of real, authentic, loving passion, to be who we are created to be.

A turning point for me when working out my identity was the ability to laugh. I am a good source of laughter. I used to feel insecure about that, but I have since embraced who I am and have come to understand that in all my mishaps, blunders, and humanness, God still loves me and wants me to laugh. If laughing really is the best medicine, I have all I need in my own bones. My tongue so often fails me, and my actions never play out as my brain tells them to. Yet I still laugh. The imperfect person I am strives every day to be more like Jesus. I choose to be part of the movement of Christ, and in that movement, I will embrace this imperfect body as I long for the one that awaits me.

My ability to laugh was tested in a unique and interesting way. My husband, four boys, one of their friends, and I were all out to eat one day when a gentleman walked over to us and told us how sweet and wonderful our family appeared. He explained that he had been watching us and was amazed at how kind the boys were to each other. He went on to say that he was the producer of a local television show and would like our family to be guests. The show would be all about us and would be called The American Family. We asked a bucketful of questions, took a few days to think about it, and then said, "Yes!" Something like this just doesn't happen to us, so we were excited that maybe we would be able to share our faith and help other families.

The day arrived. We were all dressed in our nice, yet casual, clothes. The boys were prepped on how to be good listeners and to answer any questions honestly for the duration of the taping. It seemed like all was on track.

We sat onstage, microphones on, ready for this unique adventure. The boys were sitting quietly and respectfully, and I was feeling proud. The cameraman began taping, and the host began talking. What had once been a blank, black-screened monitor now reflected the stage, so my children could see themselves on a television screen. Jacob and Levi sat motionless, too scared to move. But my two youngest, Gavin and Asher, could not stop looking at themselves in the magical screen. It was all about them.

Soon, they began exploring the stage. They threw themselves on the floor, ran around the chairs where my husband, Ashley, and I sat, and everything spiraled out of control. This was a live show, so there would be no editing of these children who were jumping all over the stage and on the leather furniture while making faces into the camera. My husband did the count to three on his fingers, which was all caught on tape. I laughed it off, trying to understand what had gone wrong. I am sure the host needed medication after that shoot.

I was mortified. I wanted to slink down in my chair and slide right off the stage. But that was clearly not how this was going to play out. At one point, my youngest son jumped into my lap, took off his shoes, put his feet in my face, and talked as loud as his little voice would let him.

The host had not signed up for this. What he saw when we were at dinner was not what he was experiencing now. But let's face it. The boys were eating then, and what boy isn't happy when eating? Maybe if they had something to eat on the set things would have turned out differently.

Finally, this unnerving experience came to a close and filming was over. Could I scream, run? How do I even apologize enough? I was unsure how to even move, so my body stayed still. I needed someone to spur me on, to say it was okay and to tell me to get up. And in that moment, someone did just that. The cameraman walked over to me and quietly said, "You did great. And just remember, they are kids."

He was right. They were kids. But I still left the studio frustrated, even defeated. I couldn't even be upset with my children; they were exactly that, children. What I did ponder was, "What will people think of me? Will others judge me because I couldn't control my boys?" I felt like a failure. How could this have gone so wrong? We should have just said no. None of this would have happened if we had turned it down to begin with.

Just when I couldn't get any lower or any more down on myself, the phone calls came in. Friends talked about how funny the show was and how real our family behaved. One person said she was so relieved because the show reflected almost every day in her home, and before that day, she felt all alone. Someone else said that they hadn't laughed like that in years. I was determined not to watch it, as I was too embarrassed to admit that it really was my family on that tape. However, a dear friend recorded the show and invited us over to view it in the safety of her home. We agreed to do so.

When we watched it, we laughed so hard tears streamed down our faces. My sides ached and cheeks hurt. It was honestly no longer embarrassing but raw, honest, and, yes, hilarious.

I realized while watching that show of a family seemingly gone wild that I was not defined by my children's behavior. I absolutely could not be defined in thirty minutes, and I would not allow myself to feel defeated. In that moment, I could either move backward and feel sorry for myself or move forward because life is real, laughter is a source of life, and we had shown exactly that. I was not going to allow my identity to be stolen, nor my joy to be robbed. Whatever came across on that screen, I knew the gentle heart of my family, and nothing else mattered.

We went on that show with a purpose, which was to reveal to others how the "American Family" looked. Afterward, it didn't feel that we had succeeded. However, after much reflection, I realized that we were exactly that. Our four boys really are great and usually well behaved, but they are children. Ashley and I are finished hiding our flaws and allowing anyone to tell us we aren't good parents because our children aren't perfect. Such things will not confine me any longer.

That label got thrown away that day. Neither my children's actions nor my circumstances would have the opportunity to change who I am. Life is too short, and Ashley and I want to enjoy every second of it and, most importantly, each other. I will take the mishaps to reach the times that are absolutely priceless. There will be moments when we must choose to laugh or cry. I will choose to laugh.

When we understand that our identity is in Christ, we are able to laugh. Find solace there, and be ready to heal. You are not a victim! You are not less than! You are not worthless! You are all the perfect things God set in motion over you. Your life has been marked with great things that only you can do. Your identity has met its match and is waking to a new day. It has been allowed to sit dormant too long, but today, in this moment, you are able to see yourself as your Savior sees you. You are able to throw off the unrighteousness and doubt and put on new clothing of worth, hope, peace, righteousness, joy, possibility, life, and movement in the gifts you have been entrusted. Your identity is now awake and alive in you and has moved strategically from death into life.

Now this is your opportunity. What you do with that new life will mark the moments to come, so make it count. Be bold and courageous. Walk into His presence, knowing you are redeemed, loved, and capable of anything. Be ready to do great things. Be ready to be obedient. Be ready for all that He has to be unleashed into your life, because you, my friend, are His. Identity is found in His Spirit. Let that wash over you. Just as Peter knew his identity was in Christ, so can you. Your identity is His promise that He will never leave you. It is by that identity that we choose to move.

Now once integrity and identity have settled into your spirit, the rest will flow like the rapids. The movement of what is to come is a product of what has preceded. The next of the "I's" is an overflow of who you are once you understand the first two positions. It is easy because now the work, you finally realize, has been done. Your debt has been paid. Instead of busying yourself being the meal-making, PTA-going, homework-doing, volunteering, at-the-end-of-your-rope-trying-to-impress soccer mom, woman, and friend, live with authentic faith and purpose and call out everything meant for you. All those aforementioned things are fine when expressed with balance. However, when they run our lives and rule our thoughts, they own us. The next "I" doesn't own us; we own it because it is built into us. Now that we understand our identity and live with integrity, the outcome of those is the third "I"—inspiration.

To inspire someone is to give them a reason to follow you. Inspiring allows you to lead from a distance. Someone can be inspired by something they hear on television or at a conference or read in a book, producing a thought or feeling one may not have known otherwise. Inspiration can come in so many ways. A picture can inspire our creativity; a person can inspire our thoughts and our visions.

But there can be a significant amount of pressure when you

inspire others. The main point of inspiration is changing the way someone thinks about something, whatever that something may be. It is where dreams are made. Inspiration has been birthed from valuable resources. We may have been inspired by our parents, teachers, or friends. Can you name someone who has inspired and even helped you change the direction of your life? Think about that person. Then think about when, why, and how he or she inspired you. What gave him or her the ability to do so? He or she was most likely someone you trusted, believed in, and felt connected to in some way.

We have friends who have three children, one of whom has type 1 diabetes. This certainly wasn't something they planned or knew from birth. This was something that just happened. William was diagnosed with diabetes when he was four and half years old, it has been a long journey for all of them. While our friends could have felt defeated and given up, they didn't. They chose to be part of a movement with power and purpose and became active in the fight against diabetes. They bike ride for William's Hope, raising money for the cure. They also run, wearing shirts to raise awareness of their cause.

Our friends don't bike or run for mere exercise; they are biking and running with a purpose. They believe their child deserves a full life, insulin free, so they will walk, run, bike, and move with absolute power to see this dream come to life. They know that no cure has ever been discovered while someone sat on the sidelines, and that hope is never birthed from someone unwilling to move. They are not giving up. They will fight as long as they have breath for the sake of their child and millions of others. My friends love their child, and nothing will stop them from pursuing a future of full health for William. And because we love them, we want to be part of the movement alongside them. We want to move for a cure. Inspired by their passion and actions, we know that we can be part of something bigger than ourselves because our focus is on the possibilities of what can be.

Inspiration changes an inspired person in a positive way. It is all around us. We can find inspiration in tangible or intangible objects. It may be something that gives life simply because the person was willing and open to see its beauty. Inspiration is always in the eye of the beholder. Find your inspiration, and then be an inspiration. Don't lose your integrity and identity because you overlooked the inspiration right in front of you. Seize it. Become a movement of God's glory.

The final "I," and the one that gives feet to everything already discussed, is influence. Influence is the power to not only inspire someone but to also bring movement into their lives. Influence is the force compelling us to act, to change our way of thinking, and to be greater than we ever thought possible. I have been blessed with two influences that changed the course of my life.

My mother was the first of those influences. As a single mom raising two children, she displayed integrity, a solid identity, and was an inspiration. At times, we lived in some not-so-familiar settings, but we never knew we had less. My mom worked harder than anyone I have ever met, making sure that our moving from a nice home in one state to a small apartment hundreds of miles away felt like an exciting adventure. She sheltered my brother and me from the reality of what was actually happening so we would have hope in our lives. She didn't allow us to become our circumstances or defined by the blows of life. She made us work hard and strive for all we were created to be. She filled me with the ability to give my dreams flight and to take action toward my goals. My mother was a faith-walking, truth-talking, Bible-believing child of God and leader of my life in many ways. She was the embodiment of love and was always moving. She showed me the purpose and power of movement within my own life because she allowed God to move through hers.

My mother was a reflection of the very heart of God. But even though she was incredible, I needed something more. So often we look to what is missing in our lives instead of to what we have. While my mother was present and involved, my father was absent and disengaged for much of my life. It was easy for him to disconnect when things didn't go his way, and he chose to move. And his movement meant the absence of a man in my life, an absence that could have determined how I viewed God, my heavenly Father. Although I often needed a map to Acceptanceville and Approval Town, I really can't blame my earthly father. I simply think he didn't know better because better was never offered to him. He was never led or given unconditional love. Now, that doesn't excuse his absence, but I do feel sorry for him. I sense his loneliness and wonder how one's pride can immobilize him for so long. No, I can't blame him. It is what he was given. But I can be grateful that things weren't easy because along the journey I have learned to forgive much, love deeply, and trust—well, I am still working on that one, but my goal is to trust completely.

The second influence on my life was a man who showed great love and integrity. So while my father was out of my life more than he was in, I looked deeply into the world of my grandfather. He was my mom's dad, but I would have claimed him as my own. I remember how he read the Bible every night and prayed with me when we visited. I remember him waking two hours every morning before everyone else and going into his private place to pray. Early one morning, I snuck downstairs to watch him on his knees, interceding for others. I am sure he prayed for those he knew and those he didn't. Even during his battle with leukemia, he never ceased praying, never felt sorry for himself, and never stopped believing in the power of a holy God. My grandfather was obedient and faithful. He knew who he was in Christ and was certainly a man of integrity.

When I was a child, my grandfather would let me stay up late after everyone else had gone to bed. We lay on the couch together watching black-and-white cowboy movies until my eyelids were too heavy to keep open. I didn't even like cowboy movies, but I didn't care. I was with him and had his big, warm arm tucked behind my neck. I would have stayed on that couch for days if it meant being by his side. That is what inspiration and influence does. They lead you where you wouldn't go by yourself and direct you to do something that, left to your own resources and devices, you would not do. My grandfather showed me more about life, faith, and purpose than any man ever had.

Funny how memories are ingrained in our mind. Some may seem purposeless, yet they stay with us. Maybe because they brought us laughter or because in that moment there was a shift in our spirit. Whatever the reason, memories are amazing, for they usually inspire and sometimes even influence us. One of those memories was of a special drink my grandpa used to make for us that to me was the best thing ever—orange juice and diet soda. I would drink that until my belly ached, and we would laugh until we cried. Grandpa's laugh was contagious; I can still hear it today even though he has been laughing with Jesus for years.

My grandfather led with purpose. He knew he was changing the course of who I would become. He knew I needed a healthy relationship with a man to show me what to expect for myself later in a husband, and he was an excellent example. He showed me more about love, sacrifice, and grace than I can measure, and he was honest and pure. Sadly, cancer took his life much too early. He left his earthly body before he was able to walk me down the aisle or before my children were around to experience his cowboy movies, crazy drinks, undeniable laugh, and faith that could move mountains.

However, I have moved because of his influence, even today, and have made few decisions in my life when I haven't asked myself first, "How would Grandpa feel about that?" My children have heard many stories about my grandpa and the man he was. His legacy lives on; his heart beats within me and his blood runs through my veins. He influenced me to believe all that God has to offer, that I have no limitations except the ones I place on myself, and that above all else my life matters because Jesus gave His life for me.

My life is not meant to be wasted. I am meant to live with integrity, to know my identity, to inspire others to be more than they ever imagined, and to influence those I come in contact with the power of movement that comes from knowing my Savior who died so I could be free to live. I am not to live just any life but one that counts for something. I pray that at the end of this journey that God has blessed me with that I will have lived in just that way.

Whether or not you have an earthly influence, you certainly have a heavenly one. God has empowered each of us and delights in and wants everything for us. Sure, we will have struggles, but the comebacks will be sweeter. This is something my mother and grandfather proved. One thing I know: While my mom touches lives with all the "I's" here on earth, her father is filling the heavens with great joy as he walks with Jesus. Laugh, Grandpa, laugh, and thank you for showing me the "I's."

8

White Pants ... Really?

The transformation of God's holiness through our faith happens when we are walking in His momentum. Let your actions flow through you with purpose. Let your words be accurate and active. When we live out an authentic, true relationship with Jesus, we see those things that were once hidden spring forth with new life. Make promises and keep them. Mean what you say, and say what you mean. Notice those things you would normally pass by. Be the change that others cannot only see but can also feel. God wants every piece of you. So look up and walk out all the faith God has birthed in you.

One day as I leisurely drove through our neighborhood, I noticed all the happenings around me. People were running, walking, cycling, mowing, talking, and driving. But what caught my eye was a slightly older-than-middle-aged woman planting beautiful red, yellow, and pink flowers in her front yard. Nothing out of the ordinary, right? Her hair was pulled back in a tight ponytail, and she looked very put together. I could tell she was one of those ladies who liked to look well kept and fresh. Nothing wrong with that. Actually, when I first saw her, I thought, "Man, I wish I looked so good when I garden." I simply look like a hot mess with sweat-saturated hair plastered to my face, old clothes, and certainly never what I saw next.

As I looked closer, more than her well-groomed appearance and jewelry-adorned arms caught my eye. This woman was wearing white pants! Not just any white pants, but crisp, clean, almost translucent white pants! I could not believe my eyes. I had to drive back by to get another look. Some may call me a stalker, but I just say that this was a moment when God was trying to speak, odd as it sounds, through white pants.

I didn't want to miss a moment of what He was saying to my heart. He said, as crisp as those white pants, "You get to be part of a revolution with powerful fearlessness and an unstoppable faith." I didn't fully understand what He was saying to me, but I do remember my next words. I shouted to the woman in white pants, "You go, girl! More power to you!" Of course, my windows were up so she couldn't hear me. There she was, surrounded by all the stain-producing materials she could get her hands on, fearlessly planting flowers in a cascade of colors while wearing white pants. She was not worried. She wore those white pants proudly.

I saw that as a metaphor for life. Even if dirt and grime surround us, the point is to not be scared to wear white pants. We are to welcome risks and the dirt because we know that those are the moments when true revolution occurs. When we take risks, we willingly walk in an unhindered, white-pant-wearing faith. It is in those moments that we see change.

We are to challenge others as well as ourselves to create a change in the world. We are capable of great things if we allow ourselves to walk outside the line of prediction and into the area where others dare not go. We can either do what is expected or become transformed and not go back to the ways of fear, doubt, and isolation. We will walk in the light that drives away the fear of the unknown. The perceived danger in the darkness is not reality.

Perception is our weakness and assumptions our demise as we look to them to reveal what is, for in reality, they reveal nothing. There is no truth in perception or assumptions. Perception lies in the eye of the beholder; how something appears depends on the viewer. Perception only becomes truth if we give it power.

Let's use the ocean as an example. If a person were swimming in the ocean simply for leisure and solitude, his goal would be to enjoy the quiet and tempered water. But what would happen if a huge wave billowed in the distance and moved toward the swimmer? He wouldn't be expecting the wave and might even become fearful, an unpleasant event in his eyes. On the other hand, what if that same giant wave came toward an experienced surfer awaiting his next big ride? The wave would then bring welcomed excitement, and the surfer would be grateful for his awesome ride.

Perception is certainly in the eye of the beholder. You and I may see things completely different. But God sees and knows the big picture and makes it all work together. He has made us different from one another and has birthed different dreams and purposes within each of us. There is a purpose within you. You must trust Him to walk it out.

God has given us truth—His truth. Perfect and honest truth that works in unity with grace and faith. God's grace isn't always warm and fuzzy. Jesus' death wasn't cute and sweet. It was painful and bitter. Why would this free gift with such love bear pain? We hurt God each day by walking in fear instead of faith. It digs deeper and bites harder than any pain we might feel. Think about this. When we offer grace to another and they refuse it, we are hurt and saddened. How much more intensely the hurt and sadness God must feel when He sent His Son to endure more pain than we can imagine and we refuse His gift and sacrifice.

We wonder when we will be called. We make frail excuses to not be our best because we are too busy or because time just isn't on our side or maybe we just aren't brave enough. Well, let me tell you a truth from a holy God. You are strong enough, smart enough, worthy enough, and good enough to make a difference in His kingdom. Excuses do little but trick our minds into believing lies about our truth. When we walk out the faith that God has breathed within us, we will want our every step to prove the existence of His grace as it moves in our actions, words, and life.

The woman in the white pants was less concerned with the dirt and more concerned with her agenda, which was planting her beautiful, flourishing flowers. She splashed reds, yellows, and pinks throughout her yard where her white pants became even more a symbol of the light ready to fill all the dark, ugly places. The woman also realized that the movement wasn't about her. She was helping the Father create beauty around her. That is what He does. He brings forth life where death tries to reside.

When you set forth a movement, it is less about you and more about Him and how you can impact others for His glory. When we move in the things of God, we move with purpose and are not concerned with the things of this world but rather the heavenly realm and changing the course of where others or we are headed.

If we all remained in our social-networking, TV-watching, game-playing mode, we would never make a change the world can see. Sure, others can read about it, and that has some merit. But what if they can see it? The movement powered inside you by the Holy Spirit can lead people to do more, be more, and want more. When we show Jesus to others, we show them the light and assist them in moving away from darkness. We extend our hand and call them into all that awaits them.

Living in a media-frenzied society, it is easy to feel a lack of purpose and an inability to measure up on any level. Swallowed up, we lose sight of the "God picture" and focus on the fact that we are not a size two, do not get to wear a designer gown on a red carpet, are not hilariously funny all the time, do not come from a wealthy family, and do not know what to say to cure all the pains of the world. No one tells us about the personal trainer who works with the size-two person for six hours a day, that she wears the gown because the designer wants it to be seen on the red carpet, and that she is only funny because someone wrote those lines for her. Her infinite wisdom came after days of thinking about her response, not five seconds. Yes, these images can send us immediately to the dark place filled with lies where we feel insecure and hopeless of ever bringing someone into the light.

However, the light is meant to squash the dark and the shadows that lurk around us. The light is powerful and stamps out the darkness that tries to attack, devour, grab hold of, and drag us into the abyss. There really is no power in the dark. It cannot hold you and certainly cannot own you. It is about perception. The darkness is simply that—dark. If you are sitting in a room and someone turns off the light, does anything change? The only thing that has changed is perception. Although you can no longer see the objects in the room, they are still there, just in the dark.

Yet the dark has a perceived power that can leave us

motionless and scared. We do not want to remain in the dark because we fear it will become reality. Trickery is the Enemy's tool to keep us immobile and believing that giving up is the only option. When we allow lies to fill our minds, we can lose the strength to move and can be overtaken by the ploys of the Enemy to rob our joy. We wouldn't allow someone to walk into our home and take our belongings, so why do we allow the Enemy to steal our identity? Well, no more.

Who cares what the media says we should be? That is certainly not God's Word. Let's not focus on the things that we aren't and fix our eyes on all that we are. Way to go, you size-twos! This is no slight to you. Nor will those of us who are not a size two feel bad about ourselves any longer, even though the media may tell us otherwise. We will not allow that to have authority over how we feel and will not be pulled into the darkness of believing we do not measure up.

What holds you back from the light? Maybe you already feel overwhelmed and busier than you ever imagined. Maybe your identity has been attacked. Maybe you have made poor choices and are now living with the consequences. Life is like a puzzle; each piece has a purpose. When we are placed together properly, using the gifts we have been given, the picture can be captivating. But when we operate from a place of "have to" instead of "get to," nothing seems to work, and we become scattered and uncertain. So let's understand that our identity is in Christ, that our past choices do not define us today, and that busyness is something we do to ourselves, which is usually to hide from those things we feel are too big to face.

So with the busy places, here is what I would ask. Are there things you can cut out of your life, even though it may mean making some tough decisions? Maybe you could scale down to one group instead of three; maybe one less day at the store, one less hour at work, or one less show after the kids are sleeping. I have no idea what your schedule looks like, but I am certain that most of us have a little time we could chisel out to really hear from God and the movement He has placed in our spirits. I know that throughout my life I have busied myself to the point of sheer exhaustion, some days too tired to even blink. But I realized that in order to begin a movement or to be part of something bigger than myself, I must first be intentional. So I had to cut some things out of my hectic schedule—the busyness—and allow God to speak to me, work in me, and, yes, move me. The most vital ingredient for success is willingness to surrender all that we want and embrace all that God wants. We must give up control and place our trust in a God who wants more for our lives than we could ever imagine.

Movement is not meant to add to your already hair-raising, crazy schedule. It is meant to propel you into a place you were meant to be, which, in His plan, will be a place of peace. God has an intention of prosperity and direction for your life. He doesn't mean for you to busy yourself with all the things that hold you back from an authentic relationship with Him. We often use these things to not to think about the next bill we can't pay or the fight we had that morning or how our child has been making some not-so-wise choices lately. But we are actually operating in fear and denial. These are the moments we must own, acknowledge, and move past.

This is like a rundown gas station on what feels like an endless road trip to nothingness. You have to stop because your body can only take so much, but the scenery isn't that great and is even a bit scary. Although it serves a purpose to work things out, you stay only a short time because you think the road ahead is better than the one you are on, even if you can't see the destination. You want to get back out on the road as soon as possible because you still have a lot of ground to cover. But when you work out the pain buried deep inside that has held you back, you are freed to get back on the road and start gaining new ground. It's like that old gas station: It isn't your favorite place to stop and you may want to ignore it, but until you deal with those things that oppress you, you will not reach your destination because you won't have enough fuel to move forward.

Someone told me once that I was like a cistern because I was always going. I was working, taking children to and from school, toting them to sporting practices, art classes, music lessons, and whatever else piqued my children's interest. We had people in our home for dinners or group meetings. I did projects and helped with homework and went to all the birthday parties and games and on field trips. Busy didn't even describe my life. Moving all the time, never stopping, helping those I could.

Funny thing is, while I was always moving, I wasn't in a movement. God showed me that truth through the word He laid on someone else's heart for me. I was tired and empty and realized that either my motives had to change or my schedule did. My children shouldn't have to go without because I couldn't get myself together. I was doing many of those things because I thought it made me look like a better mom in the world's eyes. I was often lost in the lie that if I did more for others, God would trust my heart. Instead, God told me to slow down because He knew my heart couldn't be trusted on its own. While my children were certainly a movement in my life and always will be, God wanted to me to see something else that He was laying before me. He was waiting for me to look up and seek His next move over my life. I heard Him and knew I was finally shedding my old self and ready to clothe myself in the righteousness that was prepared for me. God was speaking, and I was ready to listen, unwilling to be a cistern any longer.

This woman who knew me but did not know the secret places in my life said I was a holding tank. My thoughts went straight to the fact that, even while busy, I was stale and stagnant. The odor of a cistern is offensive, as life-sucking organisms take up residence. Cisterns breed bugs that live off grime and have little purpose other than just holding the water. If nothing is moving, what is the point? The woman said that the water was ready to flow through me in a way that I couldn't stop. It would reach others, bringing life and health, running deep and wide, with a freshness that could only come from a movement of God. Cool and alive, it would move with purpose.

I got it. I was moving so much but with little to no reason behind the movement. I thought I was driving the bus, but in reality, it was driving me. The authority had shifted in my life. It became about me and what I could accomplish. I didn't know how to sit and certainly didn't know how to rest. I realized I was doing everything to make everyone else happy and also because I felt guilty if I didn't. This was clearly not a healthy way to live, and the life-sucking organisms had grown larger than I realized. I was depending on my own resources.

I forgot to ask the only One who truly mattered what His plan was. So I began seeking God and what He wanted from me. Were there areas I could say no? That was not something I did well. Could I be in a movement for God without God? Absolutely not. Here I was thinking that the good God wanted for my life was happening because I was moving all the time. However, I wasn't seeking Him, thinking about Him, or bringing Him into any of my decisions. I said God was first in my life, but I wasn't living that out in my daily life.

God showed me that my move was contrary His. I am to move in allegiance to Him and willingly in the direction He leads. He tells us to be still and listen, gives us authority to move in His righteousness, and instills in us the power and strength to see it through. When we walk in His movement, we are no longer depending on our own strength or focused on our shortcomings that the world says we have, but rather on the supernatural strength of our Father.

God's plan for our lives can feel uncertain and even scary at times. However, He promises to protect us when we walk out in abandoned obedience to His will no matter what that may be. When we lay down our will and surrender to the Father, we will encounter more movement and opportunities than we ever imagined. Our willingness is the first step toward uncovering our hiding places. Finally, we can lay down the masks we have been wearing.

In that obedience and faith lays the opportunity to rest. To sit in His presence, bow at His feet, and listen to Him as He gently whispers our next steps. When we listen, really listen, we hear God and all the goodness He has to offer. He knows our gifts because He placed them in us. He knows our skills because He has entrusted them to us. He has given us all we need to begin the journey He has laid out before us. If we rest in His presence long enough, He will give us the map, so all the directions will be clear, and we won't worry about what lies ahead but be willing to stand in great faith that only God can give. In that place we can wear our white pants and boldly walk into the dirt-filled places and pull out, fill up, and pour into all the unknowns. Maybe we can't see or even understand them, but God does and is ready to move mountains, break through crowds, and perform miracles through us.

Maybe our white pants are stained a dingy shade of gray; nonetheless, the beauty is our fearlessness to move. We can plant a harvest that produces bountiful crops. The seeds we sow are important to the harvest we reap. In our backyard, we have a small garden of blueberries, strawberries, peppers, tomatoes, and cabbage. Although it is small, it brings great joy to my children to pick strawberries from their garden, which they claim are better than any strawberries they have ever put into their mouths. I feel delight when I pick a pepper and a tomato for fajitas. Something that we helped create makes my heart smile. We planted, watered, and nurtured, and through God's sunlight, the crops grew exactly what we needed.

Isaiah 58:11 says, "The LORD will guide you always; He will satisfy your needs ... You will be like a well-watered garden, like a spring whose waters never fail." God is guiding you to move. So put on your white pants and fearless faith because God is ready to give you a harvest full of bountiful blessings.

9

Seven Thousand Miles Away

Separated by more than seven thousand miles and the vastness of the Atlantic Ocean, a father, and husband, was changing the lives of hundreds while a wife, and mother, wondered if she would be able to make it through the next two weeks in one piece. That wife was me. The only thing I was certain of during those two weeks was that someone would be changed, but I wasn't sure if it would be for the better.

As my husband developed lasting relationships, spoke to crowds, made bricks, and loved every African he could, I was holding down the fort with all the modern resources available to me. My husband had and still has an absolute, unfiltered love for the people of Africa. He has been there a few times with our church, and each time, I feel he leaves another piece of his heart there. I am so inspired by him, so in awe of his faith and enamored by his courage. He has pushed me to be better and to never settle or give up. He has led people to Jesus and has helped start programs, and the people of Africa love him. No doubt about it, he is part of a movement.

While my husband, my rock, was over seven thousand miles away, I was a mom in an urban land yet somehow stranded. He was off changing the world, and—I am going to be transparent here—I was jealous. I was holding down our home, barely holding on. Drowning in four children, work, and school, I wanted to be off changing the world. It was a tough trip. Everything that could have gone wrong did—for me, not my husband. There were no major catastrophes, but the little things added up to one huge weight.

The straw that broke the camels back happened on what seemed like a normal night. We were not at home, but my two youngest boys decided it was time to get there. We were visiting my brother and his family, who didn't live far, which meant only a quick drive home before putting my sleepy boys to bed. My mom was also leaving soon with my two oldest boys, as they were going to spend the night with her and enjoy some grandma time. Always a good thing.

Earlier that evening, the weatherman called for snow. Now this was special because we didn't see snow much in the South. We were already planning how we would decorate our snowman and the battle that would erupt in a two-on-three snowball fight. Although it was getting late, we hoped we would catch a glimpse of the white flakes falling before bed.

On our way home, Gavin, Asher, and I dreamt of all the adventures that lay in wait the following morning. However, the ringing telephone interrupted our thoughts. My mom called from my brother's letting me know that her cell phone was at our house. I told her to swing by and pick it up on her way out. We arrived home and prepared for a great night's sleep.

My youngest was tucked tightly into bed and ready to drift off into a land of sweet dreams. My other son was too anxious for bed with Grandma coming, so he took his usual position when we expected company—in the front window. He stood there, waiting to see headlights in the darkness. The outside lights were on, and he had Grandma's phone in his hand. Then we both saw the flicker of white falling from the sky. It was snowing only a little, but it was still snowing. We were so enthralled by the beauty that we almost missed the headlights.

We lived on a gated street, which meant our visitors had to punch in a code for the gate to open before they could drive through. We saw lights down the street at the gate, but the gate did not open. Why won't the gate open? I wondered. Mom couldn't call me because I had her phone. Maybe she forgot the code, or maybe it wasn't working. I had a choice to make. The falling snow thickened, so I needed to make my decision fast.

There was now a sheet of white falling from the black sky. I decided to run down the street to give my mother her phone. I had to move quickly. I threw on some shoes and told my five-year-old to stay put and watch me from the front window. He said he would, but never having been left alone before, even to walk across the street, I could tell he was nervous. I explained I needed him to be courageous, and that I would run as fast as I could.

And I did just that. Although it was only seven houses down, in the pelting snow and knowing my child was scared, it felt like an eternity. It was truly the icing on this already lesson-learning, pride-crushing, mind-boggling two weeks while my husband was away. I had to be strong. That was my job as a wife and a mother.

I reached the car, gave my mom her phone, blew kisses to my boys, told them to drive safely, and quickly began to run back. The snow was coming down so hard I could barely see in front of me. Suddenly, I heard this noise in the distance. I could not see anything, but the sound grew louder and closer. Then through the falling snow, I saw my child running toward me with his pajamas blowing in the brisk air, his shoeless feet moving as fast as they could over the snow-covered ground. I felt I was living out one of those terrible scenes in some drama.

I don't usually panic, but that night I did. I tried lifting him to carry him back home. You know, "I'm here to save the day" type moment. I was going to get to be that superhero after all.

"Don't leave me, Mommy!" he shouted. As if I would ever leave him, but I guess I did, even if only seven houses down.

As I attempted to carry him home, I collapsed and couldn't move. Limp, my body would not cooperate. What was happening? We were only three homes away, but it literally felt like three miles. I could not get us there. Maybe I was exhausted from the week, maybe anxiety had taken over, or maybe the adrenaline had wiped me out. One thing I knew for certain, however, was that my barefoot child could no longer stand in the snow as it continued to fall around us.

I picked myself up, gave a six-second pep talk, probably more for myself than for my five-year-old, and told him he was going to have to show great courage. We ran back home together, my legs shaking all the way. My heart pumped so hard I thought it would explode. I looked up, took a deep breath, and silently prayed for God to give me strength.

Once home, I towel-dried my son, feeling like a failure. I couldn't even lift my child. I was no hero. All those lies from the beyond quickly rushed over me.

I held Gavin tightly in my arms as tears streamed down my already wet face. Would he ever trust me again? Would he ever come to me to pick him up? This reminded me of God. There are times in our lives when He may not pick us up, but will we still trust in His power and goodness? It is always there, but sometimes He may tell us to walk it out instead of carry us because that is how we learn lessons. Even though God can lift us, He loves us enough to encourage us to move. My child dug deep within himself that night for courage. As we ran together, he fought the snow, and we made it back to safety.

As I held my child, I imagined how my husband would have fixed this. He would have picked him up and carried him home. But he wasn't there to do so. As I allowed the Enemy to take over my thoughts, telling me that I had failed my child, I felt guilty for making such a poor decision. Then God whispered in my ear, "In your weakness I am strong." Yes, yes! He was, is, and always will be stronger, and not only in my weakness.

God taught me something that night. I must move, but I am also responsible to encourage others to move. God showed me that through my son and, even more importantly, through His.

When my energy returned, I carried my little guy upstairs and put him in my bed where his daddy usually slept. As I watched him drift off to sleep, we were both warmed by the love of our faithful Father.

I remembered the story of the prodigal son. Of course, not the content but the context. My son and I ran toward one another with such love that even though my child was scared, once he met my embrace, he was filled with my unconditional, unwavering, immovable love as if we had never been apart. And that is how the prodigal son felt. His father adored him as our Father adores us. He wants to meet us where we are. The porch light is on, and He is waiting. So run to Him. If you need to be picked up for a season, He has all the strength you need. There is nothing you have done that He will not forgive. He is always available to hold you, clothe you, and celebrate you.

This journey can be a tough walk. You have tried hard and may feel a bit tattered along the way. Just as my child ran to me in his fear, we too can run into the arms of our Savior, Healer, and Redeemer. There are times when we all need to be refueled, nourished, loved, encouraged, and held. This is as natural as the sun rising at dawn. God wants to hold us just as we want to embrace, care, and love our own children. He is our Father and desires to fill us with all the emotional, spiritual, and physical nutrients we need.

Rest in Him. It is important to your health. When you have received the rest your body and spirit require, your next place is to move and offer that same nourishment to others. This step is in itself a movement, an act that cannot be hidden or kept, and is a refuge to other weary souls.

David was someone who knew when to rest. He also knew that it was only for a moment and then he continued to be part of the movement of God. Years ago, I studied David's strengths, accomplishments, and even his mishaps. I really wanted to know how and why he was still called "a man after God's own heart."

God stated in Acts 13 that He knew David would do anything He asked, and that inspired me. I looked deeper into the kind of leader David was and how he led movements so much larger than himself. He knew that he couldn't fully understand the greatness of God, as He was too big, too wide, too strong, too tall, and too amazing for the finite mind to grasp. But what David did know was that, no matter what, God wanted everything good for his life, and that his intentions were pure. David made mistakes and many were gigantic by human standards. But those things didn't matter to God because eventually David repented. He wasn't held back by his sins, but rather he kept moving. Not only that, he taught us what it means to help others move. David demonstrated power and purpose poured out.

In 1 Samuel 30, we find David fighting the Amalekites, a vicious group that took everything into its possession, including women and children. David's army was tired. They had fought long and hard, and although persistent and determined, they endured loss and pain. Then the Lord told David to gather his six hundred men, as this was their moment. They would win against the Amalekites and regain all they had lost. Victory would be theirs.

So David set out on a mission to charge the enemy. But there was just one problem. His men were exhausted. While traveling, they came to a brook named Besor, whose waters flowed briskly and boldly. Two hundred men could not cross Besor, for they were too worn out. The fight had been too much, and they could not go on.

What David did next set him apart. He told those two hundred men to stay at the brook and rest while the remaining four hundred went on ahead. And the two hundred did just that; they rested. The battle had raged hard against them, and they needed renewal. The brook was their refuge.

Wait. Let's look at that again. God told David to take six hundred men and he would win. He never said two hundred were going to sit out. But David never questioned how they would win now that they were only fighting with four hundred men, for he trusted God.

David might have worn white pants and moved a mountain that day. He knew that God was good and faithful. So the four hundred went off to war while the two hundred rested their battle-scarred, weary bodies.

The Bible tells us that the four hundred conquered the Amalekites, took back what was rightfully theirs, and claimed their authority through God. The four hundred men along with all their belongings and people met the two hundred men where they had left them at the edge of the brook Besor. The two hundred greeted them and all that they had reclaimed. And the Bible says that David greeted them joyfully. He was as excited to see them as they were to see him.

While David was dividing what they had recovered amongst the men, some troublemakers decided to speak, letting the true spirit of their hearts shine. They claimed that David should not give any of the spoils to the two hundred, for they did nothing but sit and therefore weren't worthy of the belongings.

David explained that this was not how they should behave. They could not be selfish and look down on the men who had stayed behind. David went on to say that all were equal. Some fought the battle while some guarded the equipment, and there was a need for both.

David reminds us that we can stay so busy fighting on the frontlines that we don't take a moment to sit and rest. Sometimes, we, too, must find respite by the brook Besor. We must see God's presence there and allow Him to fill us up. Only there can we regain our strength to get back up and continue on in battle. It allows us solace to worship and rest and to prepare for the next movement. Once we are renewed, we can bring others along with us or encourage them to pursue the movement God is birthing in them.

When life is tough and restoration feels impossible, remember to take a moment to drink from the brook Besor. God will fill you up there through His Word and His Spirit. Meet Him at the edge of the brook for the restoration of your energy. It will come as sure as the sun will set, but you must be ready. For those two hundred men who rested there, Besor would be remembered for a lifetime. Refuge and renewal are lifelines to the purpose and power of our movement.

In Psalm 16 NLT, David writes what to hold onto and what to claim in our own lives,

> Keep me safe, O God, for I have come to you for refuge.
> I said to the LORD, "You are my Master! Every good thing I have comes from you."
> The godly people in the land are my true heroes! I take pleasure in them!
> Troubles multiply for those who chase after other gods. I will not take part in their sacrifices of blood or even speak the names of their gods.
> LORD, you alone are my inheritance, my cup of blessing. You guard all that is mine.
> The land you have given me is a pleasant land. What a wonderful inheritance!
> I will bless the LORD who guides me; even at night my heart instructs me.
> I know the LORD is always with me. I will not be shaken, for he is right beside me.
> No wonder my heart is glad, and I rejoice. My body rests in safety.
> For you will not leave my soul among the dead or allow your holy one to rot in the grave.
> You will show me the way of life, granting me the joy of your presence and the pleasures of living with you forever.

David truly was a man after God's own heart. He pursued God just as God pursued Him. And although he made some big mistakes, as we do, David was willing to continue in the movement created specifically for his life.

His story encourages us. No matter what lies in our past, we too can continue. The penalty for our sins has been paid, and God's presence surrounds us with renewal. Even if we feel thousands of miles away from God or feel His plan is too crazy for our lives, He will lead us on and prepare us for whatever awaits.

We can be refreshed at brook Besor to carry on for the battle ahead. The Holy Spirit will fill and prepare us for the God-ordained movement to change lives. We are meant for big things. Expecting anything less is belittling the power, presence, and purpose of God Himself. So close the gap between your intended movement and the life you are living. Don't allow neglecting your calling be the reason for not beginning today. God pursues you. He loves you. He knows your every longing and your potential. You, too, can be a woman or man after God's own heart.

10

Attic Full

Jesus came to give us an abundant, full life. He wants our lives to spring forth with plenty and desires for us to overflow with His goodness.

> So the Word became human and made his home among us. He was full of unfailing love and faithfulness. And we have seen his glory, the glory of the Father's one and only Son. (John 1:14)
>
> Always be full of joy in the Lord. I say it again—rejoice! (Philippians 4:4)

Be full in Him. I was reminded of what that looked like one rainy day.

My son and I decided to eat an early lunch. We were more bored than hungry, so I made a big meal with pastas and fruits. We ate and talked and ate and talked. When I became very full, I stopped eating, but I sat with my four-year-old as he continued enjoying his food and laughing and talking.

Suddenly, he put his fork down, pushed his plate away, put his hand to his belly, and said, "Wow, I have to stop. I am attic full!"

I had never heard that expression before, so I asked, "What did you say?"

"I said, 'I am attic full,'" he answered. "You know, all the way to the top, just like the attic." I loved it! How clever!

I then considered what that meant in the spiritual realm. To be full, I mean, to be "attic full," can be an overwhelming thought. Do we dare open ourselves to that kind of power? To be full is to be overtaken. When we see God in His fullness, we focus on the abundance He has promised and can be overtaken by His presence, goodness, and purpose.

One thing that seemed to ring true in David's life was that he sincerely loved God with overflowing gratitude. He was so in tune with God's presence that he was literally overtaken by it. He was "attic full" of God's goodness in his life. The Bible paints a portrait in 2 Samuel 6 of David dancing with shameless abandon when he couldn't take more than six steps while carrying the ark of the covenant before he was overcome with desire to worship the Lord. He had to set down the ark and praise God. His joy was so consuming that it was uncontainable, and David danced before the Lord with all his might, unashamed. He loved God and was more than full. He was overflowing.

Through His fullness, Jesus revives and awakens our spirits. He wants us to have a refreshing newness that overwhelms us. Revival is the beginning of a change happening within the heart. When we choose to do more, be better, and accept the movement, we become transformed. Jesus made us for transformation; we were meant for change. We so often become busy with the tasks of life that we forget the revolution that is growing and ready to move us from the inside out. These things are for us and freely given to us. We must remember who we are meant to be in Christ. Jesus didn't fret over the struggles of life. He moved through and past them, staying focused on the purpose of His Father. He was not distracted or discouraged. He moved in a God movement, "attic full" of faith and hope.

Jesus changed lives with every step He took. Your movement may be to impact hundreds. Or you may be called to purposely impact only one person. When we follow the will of the Father and stand in the gap for others, we are acting out the movement. God wants us to be willing to move for one as we are for many. It is usually with the one where real, true, powerful change occurs. God believed in the one and was willing to leave the entire flock if it meant saving the lost one. In Luke 15 NLT, Jesus told a story of what losing one looked like to Him.

> If a man has a hundred sheep and one of them gets lost, what will he do? Won't he leave the ninety-nine others in the wilderness and go to search for the one that is lost until he finds it? And when he has found it, he will joyfully carry it home on his shoulders. When he arrives, he will call together his friends and neighbors, saying, "Rejoice with me because I have found my lost sheep." In the same way, there is more joy in heaven over one lost sinner who repents and returns to God than over ninety-nine others who are righteous and haven't strayed away!

We cannot forget the power of one; the power of one pouring into another one. The one matters to God, always has and always will. Today, move out of feeling worthless and into triumph. You matter!

The power and purpose of One was taken upon a cross who bore our shame on His shoulders. God's Son came to earth in the form of flesh that endured great physical pain as it was ripped and torn, beaten over and over. Not only that, He hung with the weight of the sins of the entire world and all those that were yet to come thrust upon Him. What a Savior. What a rescuer. Would He have done that for only one? Yes, I believe God's heart was and is for the one. God ignites the "one-at-a-times." Even if hundreds of his children are drawn to Him at once, He still welcomes them into His kingdom one at a time. He recognizes each heart as His.

God has given you the ability to do what He has called you to do with all that He has entrusted. So don't waste it. Don't feel neglected because you want to make a greater impact than upon the one. When you are walking in the One who designed you, you will see that it always began with one! He desires for you to be so full of the Holy Spirit that He overflows from you. Jesus wants to fill and overtake you with His presence. Allow His love to fill and overflow from your spirit. May He fill your empty places, and may you deliver health and freedom to others. The movement of God is in your hands. God wants you to be willing to be part of what He is doing.

Following is a journal entry I wrote several years ago, which I thought was applicable here and also a bit transparent. Interestingly enough, this was and is my heart, yet I am uncertain as to whether I have ever truly been full of His Spirit to the point of overflowing with shameless abandon. That is my earnest prayer: to abandon everything I want to the will of my Father.

Oh God, create in me a pure heart. One that searches You no matter in the wilderness or on the mountaintop. Help me to be open to Your calling, draw closer to You, and surrender to Your will.

Only You know my heart. May forgiveness reside there. I pray for humility to take up residence in my life. Test me in all my ways that I may be blameless before You. For You are the God of grace and the God of mercy. When all the world comes at me, help me know that You are there.

May I love as You have loved with a selfless heart and generous hands. May You guide me as I follow You.

When the world has broken me down, You bring me home with the light on and Your arms outstretched. You embrace me with Your love.

No matter how tough life can get, when everything seems to crumble around me, help me to dance like David danced. When I am walking in Your will, leaning on You with all my might, help me to dance like David danced.

In You I place my hope and trust. You promise that hope does not disappoint. Your love has been poured out. May the Holy Spirit wash over me and cleanse my heart.

Though I may not understand what You are saying, I will trust in You. When I can't see Your plan clearly, still I will trust.

God, love me through all my faults, sustain me through all my trials, make me pure in all my thoughts, and guide me in all my ways.

God is so available to us. We have the privilege to seek Him and ask Him to fill us so we can overflow with His presence. He will give us all we need to be healthy and bountiful. He desires us to be "attic full" and to have life in abundance.

When the movement of God overtakes us with such joy, our next step is to abandon everything that hinders our glowing in the presence of Jesus. Then we are "attic full" and can dance like David with all our might.

11

Between Bugs and Walls

Having four boys has led to a life of sporting events both played and watched, parks, fishing, superheroes, pillow fights, endless games of tag, dirt-painted faces, and bug-catching extravaganzas. But I wouldn't trade one moment. It will all pass by before I can catch up with all that is happening.

Some days are filled with absolute exhaustion, and some nights are filled with terror from the enemy's ploy. Tears are wiped away from falls and the hurts of life. But one thing I have learned on this journey is that my deepest desire for my children is for them to have a full, relational, and powerful life in Christ. This is something I must display for them as an example so that one day I will be one they call out as their inspiration and influence.

When my children were very young, I always said to them, "Don't bite the bed bugs." Now, we all know the actual saying is "Don't let the bed bugs bite." However, I didn't want my children to slide into bed and say an adage that invited fear to creep into the same sheets as their innocent little bodies. My heart for my children, even as they went to bed and drifted off to sleep, was for them to feel empowered. They should have authority over those bugs, especially since they were never really there to begin with. Yet the saying allows for growing thoughts of little bugs and then larger bugs to creatures moving under beds to monsters lurking in closets. That is no way for a child to rest. Fear can dictate the actions that follow.

When we live in fear, we lack movement. Fear paralyzes us and gives strength to who or what truly has none. We cannot live in fear, for it will crush our dreams and smother us. We are to live in a place of freedom and allow our Father's heart to beat in ours. God has ordained certain gifts that have been fashioned specifically for you. Your story has been written by the most amazing author who ever was, is, or will be. You were created with a unique purpose and the power to see it through.

Jesus was and is our superhero. He didn't wear a cape or a fancy mask, and I feel pretty confident that He didn't care anything about eggs. But He did come to save us and set us free from all that holds us back. He never intended for us to be held in bondage. Have you ever felt like you were moving in a certain direction but all you ever did was hit a wall? Did you feel like you couldn't keep going because the wall was too large or too strong to break through?

My husband once gave me a thought-provoking message to listen to about a wall. The gentleman stated that when we come up against a wall, we are to be glad and not give up. If we are moving closer to the wall, we are on the offensive and are moving, which is exactly what we want. People who are defensive are hiding behind the wall and are hopeless.

Immediately, the following thoughts flooded my mind. When on the defense, we are motionless. Be clear that God is not and has never been on the defense, as He does not have to defend His status, calling, placement, and, most of all, movement.

The Enemy, however, is on the defense, and his sole desire is for us to be right there with him, beating our head against the wall with nowhere to go. When on the defense for too long, our next step is death, which begins eating away at our mind, heart, and every speck of life that was trying to break free for the Son to breakthrough. Remember, defensiveness breeds carelessness. We cannot be on the defense, children of God.

If you find yourself on the defense, it is time to switch sides. It is possible, so keep pressing. The defense has a place, as in one of our favorite pastimes played out on a green field. The pig-skinned sport shows us that defense has a place, but even it wants the offense back out on the field. If the other team intercepts or takes the ball back, the defense is over. This gives them less time to gain strength, and the offense is back out on the field, ready to take back what is rightfully theirs.

I came to understand this position when one of my sons played football. He was on the offense, but I realized that even those not running the ball were still pressing in on the defense so their men could gain ground. Yes, defense has a place, but we shouldn't stay there too long. It will be an exhausting journey if all we ever do is defend. Remember the brook Besor. Seek refuge there. Take a drink of the life-filled waters so you can move to the side gaining ground. There is a way to get back on offense.

When on the offensive side, things may feel impossible or too big, but you must keep moving. There may be times when you feel beaten down by life or may need to help a loved one find his or her way to the other side of the wall. The offensive side is not always easy. It is where most of the work presides, at least in the spiritual realm.

Make no mistake, though; the defensive side is fighting for its rights, power, and breakthrough. What the Enemy doesn't know is that the defensive side won't win. It can't. God has already won the battle; we simply must keep moving. The authority rests in His hands. When on the offense, touchdowns are made and home runs are hit. It is where the balls smash into the goals and swoosh into the baskets. When on the offense, scores are made and settled. God has won the day; the Enemy has been defeated. The battle may continue, but you, child of God, have the privilege of being on the offense.

Romans 8:31-37 makes clear the care of an invincible God. "What, then, shall we say in response to these things? If God is for us, who can be against us? ... Who shall separate us from the love of Christ?... In all these things we are more than conquerors through him who loved us." We are not just conquerors (which, quite frankly, would be enough); we are more than conquerors. That means we pass over the first stage of conquering and move to regain the power we allowed the Enemy to steal from us. Satan thought that he robbed us of our destiny, but God reminded us that on this battlefield of life we will triumph. We get to take back what is ours because God is for us. He has already won!

No matter what lies ahead, God is the leader of the offensive army. He has your back and wants you to keep pressing through the wall. Not only will it break, it will crumble at the sound of His name. Yes, the offense is winning while the Enemy is exhausted and battered, without hope of ever taking what is promised to the offense. Be bold against the things that come against you. Being on the offense and following God is your destiny. He has already made a way.

When we are confined by the construction of a building, we are up against a wall. When religion says we can't do something, we are up against a wall. God intends our breakthrough to empower us. The fullness of our Hero allows us to see ourselves in all His righteousness. Don't let those things that say you can't confine you any longer. God says you can and, through Him, you will!

The offense may be hitting the wall but has a better chance of crashing through it. The defense is waiting for the offensive line to break through. So when you do move through the wall, be ready, because your movement and momentum will trample the Enemy. God is in charge. He is your leader, and movement is happening so that the Enemy will be reminded of his defeat. Move with strength and courage. God has made you victorious.

What if the idea or perception of the wall holds you back? Here's the thing. The wall has no power. Stay with me here. Remember the ocean and the darkness mentioned earlier? What if the wall looks too thick to break through? We can become frozen, immobile, and overwhelmed. Yet Matthew 19:26 tells us, "With God all things are possible" (emphasis added).

Now imagine this. What if it was simply a beautiful painting on a canvas in the form of a wall? Well, that would certainly be easy to break through, and we would feel silly if we allowed our perception to define reality. Don't let your perception of the wall stop you from the reality of it. As stated earlier, perception is not real. It cannot define who you are or tell you where you are going. Things aren't always as they seem. The Enemy wants you to lose momentum, so there will always be obstacles. But when you move with absolute purpose, you will rise up against the Enemy with all the power and authority entrusted to you by a mighty, holy God. You will be changed and brought into a new freedom.

We must charge the Enemy. We cannot give him a leg up

or a handout. In our weakness, God will be our strength. He will move on our behalf in spite of the Enemy. When God takes over, we must dig deeply to the resurrection rising. In that moment, we regain territory and reclaim our rightful place, which is our inheritance.

God speaks power to us through His Word. In 2 Corinthians 12:9, we read, " My grace is sufficient for you, for my power is made perfect in weakness." Deuteronomy 3:16 says, "Be strong and courageous. Do not fear or be in dread of them, for it is the LORD your God who goes with you. He will not leave you or forsake you." And in Luke 10:19–20, God says,

> Behold, I have given you authority to tread on serpents and scorpions, and over all the power of the enemy, and nothing shall hurt you. Nevertheless, do not rejoice in this, that the spirits are subject to you, but rejoice that your names are written in heaven.

Know there will always be a wall because the Enemy will not give up. He wants you to be weak and frail so he can destroy all that God has ordained for your life.

The journey is yours; the walls can and will come down. Don't walk in fear but rather in His perfect love, in unhindered faith, and righteous hope that could only be birthed through Jesus' death. God is for you. You were created with purpose. It is your time so don't hold back. Walk strong and tall. And above all else, walk in a movement that only God could design within you.

Be the change. Revival is driven by emotion and revolution by action, and transformation is the result of those things working together. The movement begins in you today! Rise up, and go get 'em, you giant-slaying, lion-taming, serpent-stomping, offense-moving, heat-bringing warrior and child of the King! Today is your day to break through the wall and claim your rightful place in God's kingdom. Look up and see how much He loves you.

God's movement is available to you in this very moment. Seize and experience the presence of a Holy God who intends greatness for you. Your movement is special and important. Be refreshed and refueled. Let an awakening arise in your spirit. Bind the Enemy, as he has no authority over your life, dreams, or goals. Allow the movement you were created for to take up residence in you now. Bite the bed bugs, break through the wall, and be ready for all His goodness to be released in your life. The pain and agony He endured on the cross was intended to produce beauty in you. His death was for your life.

Don't waste another moment feeling sorry for yourself, defeated, or lost. Call out your destiny; speak the same life Your Father has spoken. You have been resurrected from the ashes, revived with His spirit, and renewed by His love. So put aside everything that keeps you busy. Your Superhero has come to save the day! Throw off your excuses and escapes. You were meant for movement with purpose and power. God is ready to move! The question is, are you?